THE NEW FOLGER LIBRARY SHAKESPEARE

Designed to make Shakespeare's great plays available to all readers, the New Folger Library edition of Shakespeare's plays provides accurate texts in modern spelling and punctuation, as well as scene-by-scene action summaries, full explanatory notes, many pictures clarifying Shakespeare's language, and notes recording all significant departures from the early printed versions. Each play is prefaced by a brief introduction, by a guide to reading Shakespeare's language, and by accounts of his life and theater. Each play is followed by an annotated list of further readings and by a "Modern Perspective" written by an expert on that particular play.

Barbara A. Mowat is Director of Research *emerita* at the Folger Shakespeare Library, Consulting Editor of *Shakespeare Quarterly*, and author of *The Dramaturgy of Shakespeare's Romances* and of essays on Shakespeare's plays and their editing.

Paul Werstine is Professor of English in the Graduate School and at King's University College at Western University. He is a general editor of the New Variorum Shakespeare and author of *Early Modern Playhouse Manuscripts and the Editing of Shakespeare*, as well as many papers and essays on the printing and editing of Shakespeare's plays.

Folger Shakespeare Library

The Folger Shakespeare Library in Washington, D.C., is a privately funded research library dedicated to Shakespeare and the civilization of early modern Europe. It was founded in 1932 by Henry Clay and Emily Jordan Folger, and incorporated as part of Amherst College in Amherst, Massachusetts, one of the nation's oldest liberal arts colleges, from which Henry Folger had graduated in 1879. In addition to its role as the world's preeminent Shakespeare collection and its emergence as a leading center for Renaissance studies, the Folger Shakespeare Library offers a wide array of cultural and educational programs and services for the general public.

EDITORS

BARBARA A. MOWAT
Director of Research emerita
Folger Shakespeare Library

PAUL WERSTINE
Professor of English
King's University College at the University of
Western Ontario, Canada

FOLGER SHAKESPEARE LIBRARY

Titus Andronicus

By
WILLIAM SHAKESPEARE

EDITED BY BARBARA A. MOWAT
AND PAUL WERSTINE

SIMON & SCHUSTER PAPERBACKS
NEW YORK LONDON TORONTO SYDNEY

Simon & Schuster Paperbacks
A Division of Simon & Schuster, Inc.
1230 Avenue of the Americas
New York, NY 10020

Copyright © 2005 by The Folger Shakespeare Library

All rights reserved, including the right to reproduce this book or portions thereof in any form whatsoever. For information, address Simon & Schuster Paperbacks Subsidiary Rights Department, 1230 Avenue of the Americas, New York, NY 10020.

Washington Square Press New Folger Edition February 2005
This Simon & Schuster paperback edition July 2010

SIMON & SCHUSTER PAPERBACKS and colophon are registered trademarks of Simon & Schuster, Inc.

For information regarding special discounts for bulk purchases, please contact Simon & Schuster Special Sales at 1-866-506-1949 or business@simonandschuster.com.

The Simon & Schuster Speakers Bureau can bring authors to your live event. For more information or to book an event, contact the Simon & Schuster Speakers Bureau at 1-866-248-3049 or visit our website at www.simonspeakers.com.

Manufactured in the United States of America

15   14   13   12

ISBN 978-0-671-72292-0

From the Director of the Folger Shakespeare Library

It is hard to imagine a world without Shakespeare. Since their composition four hundred years ago, Shakespeare's plays and poems have traveled the globe, inviting those who see and read his works to make them their own.

Readers of the New Folger Editions are part of this ongoing process of "taking up Shakespeare," finding our own thoughts and feelings in language that strikes us as old or unusual and, for that very reason, new. We still struggle to keep up with a writer who could think a mile a minute, whose words paint pictures that shift like clouds. These expertly edited texts, presented here with accompanying explanatory notes and up-to-date critical essays, are distinctive because of what they do: they allow readers not simply to keep up, but to engage deeply with a writer whose works invite us to think, and think again.

These New Folger Editions of Shakespeare's plays are also special because of where they come from. The Folger Shakespeare Library in Washington, DC, where the Editions are produced, is the single greatest documentary source of Shakespeare's works. An unparalleled collection of early modern books, manuscripts, and artwork connected to Shakespeare, the Folger's holdings have been consulted extensively in the preparation of these texts. The Editions also reflect the expertise gained through the regular performance of Shakespeare's works in the Folger's Elizabethan Theater.

I want to express my deep thanks to editors Barbara Mowat and Paul Werstine for creating these indispensable editions of Shakespeare's works, which incorporate the best of textual scholarship with a richness of commentary that is both inspired and engaging. Readers who want to know more about Shakespeare and his plays can follow the paths these distinguished scholars have tread by visiting the Folger itself, where a range of physical and digital resources (available online) exist to supplement the material in these texts. I commend to you these words, and hope that they inspire.

Michael Witmore
Director, Folger Shakespeare Library

Contents

Editors' Preface

In recent years, ways of dealing with Shakespeare's texts and with the interpretation of his plays have been undergoing significant change. This edition, while retaining many of the features that have always made the Folger Shakespeare so attractive to the general reader, at the same time reflects these current ways of thinking about Shakespeare. For example, modern readers, actors, and teachers have become interested in the differences between, on the one hand, the early forms in which Shakespeare's plays were first published and, on the other hand, the forms in which editors through the centuries have presented them. In response to this interest, we have based our edition on what we consider the best early printed version of a particular play (explaining our rationale in a section called "An Introduction to This Text") and have marked our changes in the text—unobtrusively, we hope, but in such a way that the curious reader can be aware that a change has been made and can consult the "Textual Notes" to discover what appeared in the early printed version.

Current ways of looking at the plays are reflected in our brief prefaces, in many of the commentary notes, in the annotated lists of "Further Reading," and especially in each play's "Modern Perspective," an essay written by an outstanding scholar who brings to the reader his or her fresh assessment of the play in the light of today's interests and concerns.

As in the Folger Library General Reader's Shakespeare, which this edition replaces, we include explanatory notes designed to help make Shakespeare's language clearer to a modern reader, and we place the notes on the page facing the text that they explain. We also follow the earlier edition in including illustrations—of objects, of clothing, of mythological figures—from books and manuscripts in the Folger Library collection. We provide fresh accounts of the life of Shakespeare, of the publishing of his plays, and of the theaters in which his plays were performed, as well as an introduction to the text itself. We also include a section called "Reading Shakespeare's Language," in which we try to help readers learn to "break the code" of Elizabethan poetic language.

For each section of each volume, we are indebted to a host of generous experts and fellow scholars. The "Reading Shakespeare's Language" sections, for example, could not have been written had not Arthur King, of Brigham Young University, and Randall Robinson, author of *Unlocking Shakespeare's Language*, led the way in untangling Shakespearean language puzzles and shared their insights and methodologies generously with us. "Shakespeare's Life" profited by the careful reading given it by the late S. Schoenbaum; "Shakespeare's Theater" was read and strengthened by Andrew Gurr, John Astington, and William Ingram; and "The Publication of Shakespeare's Plays" is indebted to the comments of Peter W. M. Blayney. We, as editors, take sole responsibility for any errors in our editions.

We are grateful to the authors of the "Modern Perspectives"; to William Proctor Williams for many helpful conversations about this play; to Leeds Barroll and David Bevington for their generous encouragement; to the Huntington and Newberry Libraries for fellowship support; to King's University College for the grants it has provided to Paul Werstine; to the Social Sciences and Humanities Research Council of Canada, which provided him with a Research Time Stipend for 1990–91; to R. J. Shroyer of the University of Western Ontario for essential computer support; to Chris Gray for timely help; to the Folger Institute's Center for Shakespeare Studies for its sponsorship of a workshop on "Shakespeare's Texts for Students and Teachers" (funded by the National Endowment for the Humanities and led by Richard Knowles of the University of Wisconsin), a workshop from which we learned an enormous amount about what is wanted by college and high-school teachers of Shakespeare today; to Alice Falk for her expert copyediting; and especially to Stephen Llano, our production editor at Washington Square Press.

Our biggest debt is to the Folger Shakespeare Library—to Gail Kern Paster, Director of the Library, whose interest and support are unfailing, and to Werner Gundersheimer, the Library's Director from 1984 to 2002, who made possible our edition; to Deborah Curren-Aquino, who provides extensive editorial and production support; to Jean Miller, the Library's former Art Curator, who combs the Library holdings for illustrations, and to Julie Ainsworth, Head of the Photography Department, who carefully photographs them; to Peggy O'Brien, former Director of Education at the Folger and now Director of Education Programs at the Corporation for Public Broadcasting, who gave us expert advice about the needs being expressed by Shakespeare teachers and students (and to Martha Christian and other "master teachers" who used our texts in manuscript in their classrooms); to Allan Shnerson and Mary Bloodworth for their expert computer support; to the staff of the Academic Programs Division, especially Solvei Robertson (whose help is crucial), Mary Tonkinson, Kathleen Lynch, Carol Brobeck, Liz Pohland, Owen Williams, and Dan Busey; and, finally, to the generously supportive staff of the Library's Reading Room.

Barbara A. Mowat and Paul Werstine

THE
MOST LA-
mentable Romaine
Tragedie of Titus Andronicus:

As it was Plaide by the Right Ho-
nourable the Earle of *Darbie*, Earle of *Pembrooke*,
and Earle of *Sussex* their Seruants.

LONDON,
Printed by Iohn Danter, and are
to be sold by *Edward White* & *Thomas Millington*,
at the little North doore of Paules at the
signe of the Gunne,
1594.

Title page of the 1594 Quarto.
(From the Folger Library collection.)

Shakespeare's *Titus Andronicus*

Titus Andronicus is the earliest tragedy and the earliest Roman play attributed to Shakespeare. Its tragic hero Titus acts in many ways as the model Roman, even though he makes a series of tragic errors. As the play begins, his loyalty to the Roman state is absolute, and he has given evidence of this civic virtue in his triumphs on the battlefield and in his willingness to spend his own blood in the service of extending and preserving the empire. He has led twenty-one of his twenty-five sons to death in Rome's wars. In having done so, Titus may seem to lack a feature of Roman manhood that was also highly valued, namely, patriarchal devotion to his family. This impression appears confirmed when early in the play Titus stabs to death one of his few surviving sons, who, in Titus's judgment, is showing disloyalty to Rome by resisting the desire of its newly crowned emperor.

Yet before the play is half over, Titus has come to appreciate that under the sway of the new emperor Saturninus and his bride Tamora, Rome has become "a wilderness of tigers" and that "tigers must prey, and Rome affords no prey / But me and mine." He is brought to this recognition by the death sentence imposed on two of his three remaining sons, a sentence that teaches him that the Roman tribunes are "more hard than stones." Almost immediately he is faced with the terrible rape and mutilation suffered by his only daughter. With his realization that justice has fled from Rome and that his and his family's sacrifices are now as nothing, Titus turns his fierce loyalty away from the state and toward his family alone. Many scenes in the latter half of the play show him in the company of his brother, daughter, and grandson, a foursome totally devoted to each other and joined in mutual compassion for the family's horrible suffering.

The transference of Titus's emotions from state to family is oddly mirrored in the transformation of another of the play's chief characters, Aaron the Moor. Beginning the play as its magnificent villain and the secret lover of the new empress of Rome, Tamora, Aaron seems almost to embody the near-comic figure of the Vice from drama before Shakespeare. Like the Vice, who was closely modeled on the devil of Christian theology, Aaron is nearly superhumanly inventive and resourceful in devising plots to destroy others, and, like the Vice, he takes huge delight in the destruction. Yet once the Empress, to her horror, bears him a child who is the image of himself, he turns his boundless energy and resourcefulness to the preservation of the baby, for whose sake he is ready to endure any suffering. Aaron does not lose his thirst for perpetrating evil, but he strangely combines his consummate villainy with great tenderness to his own little family—a tenderness that also comes to characterize Titus before the play reaches its terrifying conclusion.

After you have read *Titus Andronicus,* we invite you to read the essay printed after it, "*Titus Andronicus:* A Modern Perspective," written by Professor Alexander Leggatt of the University of Toronto.

Reading Shakespeare's Language: *Titus Andronicus*

For many people today, reading Shakespeare's language can be a problem—but it is a problem that can be solved. Those who have studied Latin (or even French or German or Spanish), and those who are used to reading poetry, will have little difficulty understanding the language of Shakespeare's poetic drama. Others, though, need to develop the skills of untangling unusual sentence structures and of recognizing and understanding poetic compressions, omissions, and wordplay. And even those skilled in reading unusual sentence structures may have occasional trouble with Shakespeare's words. Four hundred years of "static" intervene between his speaking and our hearing. Most of his immense vocabulary is still in use, but a few of his words are no longer used and many of his words now have meanings quite different from those they had in the sixteenth and seventeenth centuries. In the theater, most of these difficulties are solved for us by actors who study the language and articulate it for us so that the essential meaning is heard—or, when combined with stage action, is at least *felt*. When we are reading on our own, we must do what each actor does: go over the lines (often with a dictionary close at hand) until the puzzles are solved and the lines yield up their poetry and the characters speak in words and phrases that are, suddenly, rewarding and wonderfully memorable.

Shakespeare's Words

As you begin to read the opening scenes of a play by
Shakespeare, you may notice occasional unfamiliar
words. Some are unfamiliar simply because we no
longer use them. In the opening scene of *Titus Andronicus,* for example, one finds the words *larums* (i.e., calls
to arms), *avaunt* (i.e., be gone), and *affy* (i.e., put one's
trust in). Words of this kind are explained in notes to
the text and will become familiar the more of Shakespeare's plays you read.

In *Titus Andronicus,* as in all of Shakespeare's writing, more problematic are the words that are still in
use but that now have a different meaning. In the
opening scenes of *Titus Andronicus,* for example, the
word *successive* is used where we would say "hereditary," *trump* where we would say "trumpet," *forfend*
where we would say "forbid," and *bandy* where we
would say "fight." Such words will be explained in the
notes to the text, but they, too, will become familiar as
you continue to read Shakespeare's language.

Some words are strange not because of the "static"
introduced by changes in language over the past centuries but because these are words that Shakespeare is
using to build a dramatic world that has its own space,
time, and history. In the opening scene of *Titus Andronicus,* for example, Shakespeare quickly constructs a
recent background history of Rome and, more specifically, of the "Andronici," the family of "renownèd Titus
flourishing in arms." As two sons of the late Roman
emperor, Saturninus and Bassianus, "strive by factions
and by friends" for "the imperial diadem of Rome," Titus
has been "accited home," having "circumscribèd with his
sword / And brought to yoke the enemies of Rome." This
was his fifth war in ten years, a period over which he has
lost in combat all but four "of five-and-twenty valiant
sons." "To gratify the good Andronicus / And gratulate his

safe return to Rome, / The people" offer to "accept whom he admits" to "rule and empery." Such language quickly constructs the world inhabited by Titus Andronicus and his family, a world that mixes legendary Roman history with deliberately horrific tragedy of blood, a genre fashioned by the Roman tragedian Seneca; the words and the world they create will become increasingly familiar as you get further into the play.

Shakespeare's Sentences

In an English sentence, meaning is quite dependent on the place given each word. "The dog bit the boy" and "The boy bit the dog" mean very different things, even though the individual words are the same. Because English places such importance on the positions of words in sentences, on the way words are arranged, unusual arrangements can puzzle a reader. Shakespeare frequently shifts his sentences away from "normal" English arrangements—often to create the rhythm he seeks, sometimes to use a line's poetic rhythm to emphasize a particular word, sometimes to give a character his or her own speech patterns or to allow the character to speak in a special way. When we attend a good performance of the play, the actors will have worked out the sentence structures and will articulate the sentences so that the meaning is clear. When reading the play, we need to do as the actor does: that is, when puzzled by a character's speech, check to see if words are being presented in an unusual sequence.

Often Shakespeare rearranges subjects and verbs (i.e., instead of "He goes" we find "Goes he"). In *Titus Andronicus*, when Marcus announces "Returns the good Andronicus to Rome" (1.1.37), he is using such a construction. So is Titus when he says "Here lurks no treason . . . , / Here grow no damnèd drugs; here are no

storms" (153–54). The "normal" order would be "Andronicus returns" and "no treason lurks here, no damned
drugs grow here, no storms are here." Shakespeare also
frequently places the object before or between the subject
and verb (i.e., instead of "I hit him," we might find "Him
I hit" or "I him hit"). Titus provides an example of the
first kind of this inversion when he says "this suit I make"
(1.1.225) and an example of the second kind when he
says of Rome "A better head her glorious body fits" (187).
The "normal" order would be "I make this suit" and "A
better head fits her glorious body."

Inversions are not the only unusual sentence structures in Shakespeare's language. Often in his sentences
words that would normally appear together are separated from each other. Again, this is often done to create a particular rhythm or to stress a particular word,
or else to draw attention to a needed piece of information. Take, for example, Marcus's

> Titus Andronicus, the people of Rome,
> Whose friend in justice thou hast ever been,
> Send thee by me, their tribune and their trust,
> This palliament of white and spotless hue[.]
>   (1.1.179–82)

Here the subject ("the people of Rome") is separated
from its verb ("send") by the subject's modifier
"Whose friend in justice thou hast ever been." The
verb ("send") is also separated from its object ("this
palliament") by both its indirect object ("thee") and
the adverb phrase "by me," which is continued in the
appositive "their tribune and their trust." Each of
the two prominent interruptions serves to identify
the sentence with performance of the civic ritual in
which the people's tribune exercises the authority he
derives from them as "their tribune and their trust"
by identifying their choice of candidate for emperor,

who has been selected for his merits as the people's longtime "friend in justice." Or take the Captain's lines to the Roman people:

> The good Andronicus,
> Patron of virtue, Rome's best champion,
> Successful in the battles that he fights,
> With honor and with fortune is returned[.]
> (1.1.64–67)

Here the subject and verb ("the good Andronicus . . . is returned") are separated by two appositives ("patron of virtue" and "Rome's best champion") and by the appositives' modifier ("successful in the battles that he fights"—an adjective modified by an adverbial phrase that concludes by incorporating an adjectival clause), as well as by two adverbial phrases ("with honor and with fortune"). All these interruptions emphasize Titus's glorious civic virtue and military honor. In order to create sentences that seem more like the English of everyday speech, one can rearrange the words, putting together the word clusters ("the people of Rome send this palliament," "Andronicus is returned"). The result will usually be an increase in clarity but a loss of rhythm or a shift in emphasis, or, in this case, the omission of descriptors needed for the plot (and needed by the audience).

Often in *Titus Andronicus*, rather than separating basic sentence elements, Shakespeare simply holds them back, delaying them until other material to which he wants to give greater emphasis has been presented. Shakespeare puts this kind of construction in the mouth of Titus when he first comes on stage:

> Lo, as the bark that hath discharged his fraught
> Returns with precious lading to the bay
> From whence at first she weighed her anchorage,

Cometh Andronicus, bound with laurel boughs,
To resalute his country with his tears,
Tears of true joy for his return to Rome.

(1.1.71–76)

The basic sentence elements (an inversion of "Andronicus cometh") are here delayed while Titus develops the
first half of a simile on a scale that nearly rivals those
found in epic poetry. If one reverses the order, placing
the basic sentence elements at the beginning of the
sentence, the simile becomes anticlimactic, and one
sees the power of Shakespeare's delaying strategy.

Finally, in many of Shakespeare's plays, sentences
are sometimes complicated not because of unusual
structures or interruptions but because Shakespeare
omits words and parts of words that English sentences
normally require. (In conversation, we, too, often omit
words. We say, "Heard from him yet?" and our hearer
supplies the missing "Have you.") Frequent reading of
Shakespeare—and of other poets—trains us to supply
such missing words. When, for example, Saturninus
tells Titus that "no, the Emperor needs her not, / Nor
her, nor thee, nor any of thy stock" (1.1.305–6), we can
easily draw on words contained in the first line to supply the words he omits in the second line: "no, the
Emperor needs her not, / [; no, the Emperor needs] nor
[i.e., neither] her, nor you, nor any of your stock."
Again, when Titus asks two successive questions of the
Roman people, he leaves out some of the words in his
second question:

What, should I don this robe and trouble you?
Be chosen with proclamations today,
Tomorrow yield up rule, resign my life,
And set abroad new business for you all?

(1.1.189–93)

We can easily find the words needed to complete the second question from our reading of the first question. Thus we can read the second to say: "[Should I] be chosen with proclamations today . . . ?" Finally, Bassianus's radically elliptical speech "Tribunes, and me, a poor competitor" may defy sense when it is taken out of context (1.1.63). But in the play we find this speech directly after Saturninus's request "Open the gates and let me in"; we thus can quickly understand that Bassianus says "Tribunes, [open the gates] and [let] me, a poor competitor [i.e., rival] in [too]."

Shakespearean Wordplay

Shakespeare plays with language so often and so variously that entire books are written on the topic. Here we will mention only two kinds of wordplay, metaphors and allusions. A metaphor is a play on words in which one object or idea is expressed as if it were something else, something with which the metaphor suggests it shares common features. For instance, when Titus says of the Emperor's dismissal of him and his family "These words are razors to my wounded heart" (1.1.320), he is using metaphorical language to say that the Emperor's words of rejection cut him as if they were "razors" to his "heart," the "heart" being the traditional seat of life, of love, and of devotion. Tamora tells Titus that "Sweet mercy is nobility's true badge" (119), using another metaphor to identify an abstraction (the virtue "mercy") with a visible sign (a "badge," that is, a distinctive mark or emblem). She claims that the badge mercy can alone authenticate the "nobility"—another abstraction—of a human being. Tamora uses yet another metaphor as she pretends to counsel the Emperor to forgive Titus: "Take up this good old man, and cheer the heart / That dies in tempest of thy angry frown" (467–68). This time she elevates the significance of the Emperor's "frown" by metaphorically associating it with a great storm that flattens buildings, wrecks ships, and costs lives.

An allusion presents itself when one text or a character in it refers to another text, thereby prompting readers or listeners to reflect on the multiple ways in which the two texts may parallel each other. *Titus Andronicus* is extraordinarily rife with allusion. An early example comes when Tamora, mourning the slaughter of her son Alarbus, is comforted by Demetrius:

> Then, madam, stand resolved, but hope withal
> The selfsame gods that armed the Queen of Troy
> With opportunity of sharp revenge
> Upon the Thracian tyrant in his tent
> May favor Tamora the Queen of Goths[.]
>
> (1.1.135–39)

Demetrius here alludes to Ovid's account in the *Metamorphoses* of Hecuba, queen of legendary Troy, and suggests that Tamora's future may follow the same course. Since Demetrius's lines contain only a fragment of Ovid's story of Hecuba, Shakespeare evidently thought the story so well known in his time that the audience could be expected to supply the rest. That is, the audience could be presumed to know that like Tamora, Hecuba is the defeated queen of a defeated nation and that, like Tamora, whose son Alarbus has just been sacrificed to appease the ghosts of the dead, Hecuba lost her daughter Polyxena to precisely the same fate. As Shakespeare does make explicit, Hecuba's story concludes with revenge. Yet Shakespeare is careful to omit the detail that Hecuba's revenge was not against those who ritually slew her daughter, but against her son Polydorus's killer, "the Thracian tyrant" Polymnestor. Although the analogy between Hecuba and Tamora is therefore not quite exact, we can nonetheless read *Titus Andronicus* in light of the Hecuba allusion, and thus know that Tamora might well take her revenge on the family of Titus Andronicus. But the play's allusion to Hecuba does not stop with Tamora's quest for revenge, because as Tamora achieves her goal, Titus begins to suffer the loss of his children, and he then takes on the role of the suffering Hecuba, driven beyond despair into deadly wrath.

And the play's allusions do not stop with those to Ovid's Hecuba. Through allusion Shakespeare also weaves into the text of his play many threads from other classical texts. Most of these are associated with the rape of Titus's daughter, Lavinia, by Tamora's sons. They include Shakespeare's own narrative poem about the assault on the famously chaste Roman matron Lucrece by the son of Rome's last king, Tarquinius Superbus; the story of Appius's attack on Virginia that ends with her slaying by her own father, Virginius; and, most extensively, Ovid's version of the rape and mutilation of Philomela by her brother-in-law, King Tereus. Both the characters and the action of *Titus Andronicus* make such insistent reference to this last text that we have chosen to print a contemporary translation of it as an appendix to this edition of the play so that readers, if they choose, may weave their reading of it into their reading of the play just as Shakespeare seems to have woven his reading of Ovid into his writing of the play.

Implied Stage Action

Finally, in reading Shakespeare's plays we should always remember that what we are reading is a performance script. The dialogue is written to be spoken by actors who, at the same time, are moving, gesturing, picking up objects, weeping, shaking their fists. Some stage action is described in what are called "stage directions"; some is signaled within the dialogue itself. We must learn to be alert to such signals as we stage the play in our imaginations.

Often the dialogue offers an immediately clear indication of the action that is to accompany it. For example, when Titus addresses his son Mutius with the words "What, villain boy, / Barr'st me my way in Rome?" and Mutius, in response, cries out to his brother "Help, Lucius, help!" (1.1.295–97), there can be little doubt that this exchange is to be combined with Titus's infliction of violence on his son Mutius. Such an inference from the dialogue is confirmed by the next speech, Lucius's accusation against Titus: "In wrongful quarrel you have slain your son" (299). Thus we learn that Titus has stabbed Mutius to death. Dialogue again cues action in a straightforward way when Quintus attempts to pull Martius from a pit into which he has fallen during a hunt. "Thy hand once more," says Quintus to Martius. "I will not loose again / Till thou art here aloft or I below. / Thou canst not come to me. I come to thee" (2.3.244–46). Clearly, Quintus has failed to pull Martius out; instead Martius has pulled Quintus in. This inference is confirmed when the approaching Saturninus immediately announces that he will "see . . . what he is that now is leapt into" the "hole" (247–48).

Occasionally in *Titus Andronicus*, signals to the reader are not so clear. As Tamora pleads to Titus to spare her son Alarbus from being sacrificed—"Andronicus, stain not thy tomb with blood" (1.1.116)—it is not apparent from her words or from Titus's response to them— "Patient yourself, madam, and pardon me" (121)— whether Tamora stands or kneels as she utters her supplication, even though in classical literature, which

Shakespeare is imitating, supplicants usually kneel. Later in the same scene, however, Tamora reflects bitterly on the futility of her plea when she promises to make Titus and his sons "know what 'tis to let a queen / Kneel in the streets and beg for grace in vain" (463–64). In view of this later speech, we, as editors, feel reasonably confident that we can add to Tamora's earlier plea the stage direction "She kneels." But we place this stage direction in square half-brackets, just as we do all stage directions that we add to the early printed text, whether they are of our own creation or the work of earlier editors. We use these brackets because we recognize that editorial stage directions present only a single reading of the possibilities for action in the play, and we do not want to foreclose other interpretations that may occur to readers, whom we frankly invite to reject what is in brackets if they wish.

Caution in granting too much credence to bracketed stage directions is encouraged in this particular instance by reference to another passage in the play where a character reflects back on earlier action. This time the character is Aaron, who is recalling the time that Titus is brought the heads of his sons as well as the hand he has had cut off and sent to the Emperor to redeem his sons' lives:

> I pried [peered, spied] me through the crevice of
>   a wall
> When, for his hand, he had his two sons' heads,
> Beheld his tears, and laughed so heartily
> That both mine eyes were rainy like to his.
>   (5.1.116–19)

In this case, we did not, in the earlier scene, add a stage direction for Aaron to enter and view Titus's grief, mainly because there is a major discrepancy between Aaron's description and the scene he purports to describe, a

scene in which Titus makes much of his inability to
weep. It seems to us that Aaron may later be represent-
ing himself as more villainous than he actually was in
telling us that he laughed at tears that Titus did not shed.

Practice in reading the language of stage action
repays one many times over when one reaches scenes
heavily dependent on stage business. Such a scene is 4.1,
in which Lavinia uses a copy of Ovid's *Metamorphoses* to
communicate to her family that she, like Philomela in
Ovid's book, was raped and subsequently mutilated by
her assailants. The earliest printing of the play contains a
stage direction at the beginning of the scene that tells us
that Young Lucius comes onstage "with his books under
his arm." After that stage direction, we, both readers and
editors, have to depend on the dialogue alone to follow
the action. By line 25, we learn that Lavinia's pursuit of
Young Lucius has been so insistent that it has "made
[him] down to throw [his] books and fly," although we do
not know precisely when in the scene he has done so.
Then we learn from Titus's question "what book is that
she tosseth so?" that Lavinia is searching through a book
(42). Young Lucius then identifies the book as "Ovid's
Metamorphosis," the title of Arthur Golding's 1567 English translation, and one of the play's many anachro-
nisms. Finally, Titus observes that Lavinia has opened
the book to "the tragic tale of Philomel" and infers that
"rape . . . was root of [Lavinia's] annoy" (43, 49, 51). In
sum, then we learn that Lavinia has been chasing Young
Lucius to get his copy of the *Metamorphosis*, which she
opens to the story of Philomela's rape so as to show her
family what happened to her. We as editors have sup-
plied no additional bracketed stage directions to this part
of the scene, depending on readers to follow action that
the dialogue makes so clear. Throughout this text, we
have chosen not to add many stage directions found in
other modern editions in order to leave readers free to
imagine the staging for themselves.

It is immensely rewarding to work carefully with Shakespeare's language—with the words, the sentences, the wordplay, and the implied stage action—as readers for the past four centuries have discovered. It may be more pleasurable to attend a good performance of a play—though not everyone has thought so. But the joy of being able to stage one of Shakespeare's plays in one's imagination, to return to passages that continue to yield further meanings (or further questions) the more one reads them—these are pleasures that, for many, rival (or at least augment) those of the performed text, and certainly make it worth considerable effort to "break the code" of Elizabethan poetic drama and let free the remarkable language that makes up a Shakespeare text.

Shakespeare's Life

Surviving documents that give us glimpses into the life of William Shakespeare show us a playwright, poet, and actor who grew up in the market town of Stratford-upon-Avon, spent his professional life in London, and returned to Stratford a wealthy land-owner. He was born in April 1564, died in April 1616, and is buried inside the chancel of Holy Trinity Church in Stratford.

We wish we could know more about the life of the world's greatest dramatist. His plays and poems are testaments to his wide reading—especially to his knowledge of Virgil, Ovid, Plutarch, Holinshed's *Chronicles*, and the Bible—and to his mastery of the English language, but we can only speculate about his education. We know that the King's New School in Stratford-upon-Avon was considered excellent. The school was one of the English "grammar schools" established to educate young men, primarily in Latin grammar and literature. As in other schools of the time, students began their studies at the age of four or five in the attached "petty school," and there learned to read and write in English, studying primarily the catechism from the Book of Common Prayer. After two years in the petty school, students entered the lower form (grade) of the grammar school, where they began the serious study of Latin grammar and Latin texts that would occupy most of the remainder of their school days. (Several Latin texts that Shakespeare used repeatedly in writing his plays and poems were texts that schoolboys memorized and recited.) Latin comedies were introduced early in the lower form; in the upper form, which the boys entered at age ten or eleven, students wrote their own Latin orations and declamations, studied Latin historians and rhetoricians, and began the study of Greek using the Greek New Testament.

Since the records of the Stratford "grammar school" do not survive, we cannot prove that William Shakespeare attended the school; however, every indication (his father's position as an alderman and bailiff of Stratford, the playwright's own knowledge of the Latin classics, scenes in the plays that recall grammar-school experiences—for example, *The Merry Wives of Windsor*, 4.1) suggests that he did. We also lack generally accepted documentation about Shakespeare's life after his schooling ended and his professional life in London began. His marriage in 1582 (at age eighteen) to Anne Hathaway and the subsequent births of his daughter Susanna (1583) and the twins Judith and Hamnet (1585) are recorded, but how he supported himself and where he lived are not known. Nor do we know when and why he left Stratford for the London theatrical world, nor how he rose to be the important figure in that world that he had become by the early 1590s.

We do know that by 1592 he had achieved some prominence in London as both an actor and a playwright. In that year was published a book by the playwright Robert Greene attacking an actor who had the audacity to write blank-verse drama and who was "in his own conceit [i.e., opinion] the only Shake-scene in a country." Since Greene's attack includes a parody of a line from one of Shakespeare's early plays, there is little doubt that it is Shakespeare to whom he refers, a "Shake-scene" who had aroused Greene's fury by successfully competing with university-educated dramatists like Greene himself. It was in 1593 that Shakespeare became a published poet. In that year he published his long narrative poem *Venus and Adonis;* in 1594, he followed it with *The Rape of Lucrece.* Both poems were dedicated to the young earl of Southampton (Henry Wriothesley), who may have become Shakespeare's patron.

It seems no coincidence that Shakespeare wrote these narrative poems at a time when the theaters were closed because of the plague, a contagious epidemic disease that devastated the population of London. When the theaters reopened in 1594, Shakespeare apparently resumed his double career of actor and playwright and began his long (and seemingly profitable) service as an acting-company shareholder. Records for December of 1594 show him to be a leading member of the Lord Chamberlain's Men. It was this company of actors, later named the King's Men, for whom he would be a principal actor, dramatist, and shareholder for the rest of his career.

So far as we can tell, that career spanned about twenty years. In the 1590s, he wrote his plays on English history as well as several comedies and at least two tragedies (*Titus Andronicus* and *Romeo and Juliet*). These histories, comedies, and tragedies are the plays credited to him in 1598 in a work, *Palladis Tamia,* that in one chapter compares English writers with "Greek, Latin, and Italian Poets." There the author, Francis Meres, claims that Shakespeare is comparable to the Latin dramatists Seneca for tragedy and Plautus for comedy, and calls him "the most excellent in both kinds for the stage." He also names him "Mellifluous and honey-tongued Shakespeare": "I say," writes Meres, "that the Muses would speak with Shakespeare's fine filed phrase, if they would speak English." Since Meres also mentions Shakespeare's "sugared sonnets among his private friends," it is assumed that many of Shakespeare's sonnets (not published until 1609) were also written in the 1590s.

In 1599, Shakespeare's company built a theater for themselves across the river from London, naming it the Globe. The plays that are considered by many to be Shakespeare's major tragedies (*Hamlet, Othello, King Lear,* and *Macbeth*) were written while the company was resident in this theater, as were such comedies as *Twelfth Night* and *Measure for Measure*. Many of Shakespeare's plays were performed at court (both for Queen Elizabeth I and, after her death in 1603, for King James I), some were presented at the Inns of Court (the residences of London's legal societies), and some were doubtless performed in other towns, at the universities, and at great houses when the King's Men went on tour; otherwise, his plays from 1599 to 1608 were, so far as we know, performed only at the Globe. Between 1608 and 1612, Shakespeare wrote several plays—among them *The Winter's Tale* and *The Tempest*—presumably for the company's new indoor Blackfriars theater, though the plays seem to have been performed also at the Globe and at court. Surviving documents describe a performance of *The Winter's Tale* in 1611 at the Globe, for example, and performances of *The Tempest* in 1611 and 1613 at the royal palace of Whitehall.

Shakespeare wrote very little after 1612, the year in which he probably wrote *King Henry VIII*. (It was at a performance of *Henry VIII* in 1613 that the Globe caught fire and burned to the ground.) Sometime between 1610 and 1613 he seems to have returned to live in Stratford-upon-Avon, where he owned a large house and considerable property, and where his wife and his two daughters and their husbands lived. (His son Hamnet had died in 1596.) During his professional years in London, Shakespeare had presumably derived income from the acting company's profits as well as from his own career as an actor, from the sale of his play manuscripts to the acting company, and, after 1599, from his shares as an owner of the Globe. It was presumably that income, carefully invested in land and other property, which made him the wealthy man that surviving documents show him to have become. It is also assumed that William Shakespeare's growing wealth and reputation played some part in inclining the crown, in 1596, to grant John Shakespeare, William's father, the coat of arms that he had so long sought. William Shakespeare died in Stratford on April 23, 1616 (according to the epitaph carved under his bust in Holy Trinity Church) and was buried on April 25. Seven years after his death, his collected plays were published as *Mr. William Shakespeares Comedies, Histories, & Tragedies* (the work now known as the First Folio).

The years in which Shakespeare wrote were among the most exciting in English history. Intellectually, the discovery, translation, and printing of Greek and Roman classics were making available a set of works and world-views that interacted complexly with Christian texts and beliefs. The result was a questioning, a vital intellectual ferment, that provided energy for the period's amazing dramatic and literary output and that fed directly into Shakespeare's plays. The Ghost in *Hamlet*, for example, is wonderfully complicated in part because he is a figure from Roman tragedy—the spirit of the dead returning to seek revenge—who at the same time inhabits a Christian hell (or purgatory); Hamlet's description of humankind reflects at one moment the Neoplatonic wonderment at mankind ("What a piece of work is a man!") and, at the next, the Christian disparagement of human sinners ("And yet, to me, what is this quintessence of dust?").

As intellectual horizons expanded, so also did geographical and cosmological horizons. New worlds—both North and South America—were explored, and in them were found human beings who lived and worshiped in ways radically different from those of Renaissance Europeans and Englishmen. The universe during these years also seemed to shift and expand. Copernicus had earlier theorized that the earth was not the center of the cosmos but revolved as a planet around the sun. Galileo's telescope, created in 1609, allowed scientists to see that Copernicus had been correct; the universe was not organized with the earth at the center, nor was it so nicely circumscribed as people had, until that time, thought. In terms of expanding horizons, the impact of these discoveries on people's beliefs—religious, scientific, and philosophical—cannot be overstated.

London, too, rapidly expanded and changed during the years (from the early 1590s to around 1610) that Shakespeare lived there. London—the center of England's government, its economy, its royal court, its overseas trade—was, during these years, becoming an exciting metropolis, drawing to it thousands of new citizens every year. Troubled by overcrowding, by poverty, by recurring epidemics of the plague, London was also a mecca for the wealthy and the aristocratic, and for those who sought advancement at court, or power in government or finance or trade. One hears in Shakespeare's plays the voices of London—the struggles for power, the fear of venereal disease, the language of buying and selling. One hears as well the voices of Stratford-upon-Avon—references to the nearby Forest of Arden, to sheepherding, to small-town gossip, to village fairs and markets. Part of the richness of Shakespeare's work is the influence felt there of the various worlds in which he lived: the world of metropolitan London, the world of small-town and rural England, the world of the theater, and the worlds of craftsmen and shepherds.

That Shakespeare inhabited such worlds we know from surviving London and Stratford documents, as well as from the evidence of the plays and poems themselves. From such records we can sketch the dramatist's life. We know from his works that he was a voracious reader. We know from legal and business documents that he was a multifaceted theater man who became a wealthy landowner. We know a bit about his family life and a fair amount about his legal and financial dealings. Most scholars today depend upon such evidence as they draw their picture of the world's greatest playwright. Such, however, has not always been the case. Until the late eighteenth century, the William Shakespeare who lived in most biographies was the creation of legend and tradition. This was the Shakespeare who was supposedly caught poaching deer at Charlecote, the estate of Sir Thomas Lucy close by Stratford; this was the Shakespeare who fled from Sir Thomas's vengeance and made his way in London by taking care of horses outside a playhouse; this was the Shakespeare who reportedly could barely read but whose natural gifts were extraordinary, whose father was a butcher who allowed his gifted son sometimes to help in the butcher shop, where William supposedly killed calves "in a high style," making a speech for the occasion. It was this legendary William Shakespeare whose Falstaff (in *1* and *2 Henry IV*) so pleased Queen Elizabeth that she demanded a play about Falstaff in love, and demanded that it be written in fourteen days (hence the existence of *The Merry Wives of Windsor*). It was this legendary Shakespeare who reached the top of his acting career in the roles of the Ghost in *Hamlet* and old Adam in *As You Like It*—and who died of a fever contracted by drinking too hard at "a merry meeting" with the poets Michael Drayton and Ben Jonson. This legendary Shakespeare is a rambunctious, undisciplined man, as attractively "wild" as his plays were seen by earlier generations to be. Unfortunately, there is no trace of evidence to support these wonderful stories.

Perhaps in response to the disreputable Shakespeare of legend—or perhaps in response to the fragmentary and, for some, all-too-ordinary Shakespeare documented by surviving records—some people since the mid–nineteenth century have argued that William Shakespeare could not have written the plays that bear his name. These persons have put forward some dozen names as more likely authors, among them Queen Elizabeth, Sir Francis Bacon, Edward de Vere (earl of Oxford), and Christopher Marlowe. Such attempts to find what for these people is a more believable author of the plays is a tribute to the regard in which the plays are held. Unfortunately for their claims, the documents that exist that provide evidence for the facts of Shakespeare's life tie him inextricably to the body of plays and poems that bear his name. Unlikely as it seems to those who want the works to have been written by an aristocrat, a university graduate, or an "important" person, the plays and poems seem clearly to have been produced by a man from Stratford-upon-Avon with a very good "grammar-school" education and a life of experience in London and in the world of the London theater. How this particular man produced the works that dominate the cultures of much of the world almost four hundred years after his death is one of life's mysteries—and one that will continue to tease our imaginations as we continue to delight in his plays and poems.

Shakespeare's Theater

The actors of Shakespeare's time performed plays in a great variety of locations. They played at court (that is, in the great halls of such royal residences as Whitehall, Hampton Court, and Greenwich); they played in halls at the universities of Oxford and Cambridge, and at the Inns of Court (the residences in London of the legal societies); and they also played in the private houses of great lords and civic officials. Sometimes acting companies went on tour from London into the provinces, often (but not only) when outbreaks of bubonic plague in the capital forced the closing of theaters to reduce the possibility of contagion in crowded audiences. In the provinces the actors usually staged their plays in churches (until around 1600) or in guildhalls. Though surviving records show only a handful of occasions when actors played at inns while on tour, London inns were important playing places up until the 1590s.

The building of theaters in London had begun only shortly before Shakespeare wrote his first plays in the 1590s. These theaters were of two kinds: outdoor or public playhouses that could accommodate large numbers of playgoers, and indoor or private theaters for much smaller audiences. What is usually regarded as the first London outdoor public playhouse was called simply the Theatre. James Burbage—the father of Richard Burbage, who was perhaps the most famous actor in Shakespeare's company—built it in 1576 in an area north of the city of London called Shoreditch. Among the more famous of the other public playhouses that capitalized on the new fashion were the Curtain and the Fortune (both also built north of the city), the Rose, the Swan, the Globe, and the Hope (all located on the Bankside, a region just across the Thames south of the city of London). All these playhouses had to be built outside the jurisdiction of the city of London because many civic officials were hostile to the performance of drama and repeatedly petitioned the royal council to abolish it.

The theaters erected on the Bankside (a region under the authority of the Church of England, whose head was the monarch) shared the neighborhood with houses of prostitution and with the Paris Garden, where the blood sports of bearbaiting and bullbaiting were carried on. There may have been no clear distinction between playhouses and buildings for such sports, for the Hope was used for both plays and baiting, and Philip Henslowe, owner of the Rose and, later, partner in the ownership of the Fortune, was also a partner in a monopoly on baiting. All these forms of entertainment were easily accessible to Londoners by boat across the Thames or over London Bridge.

Evidently Shakespeare's company prospered on the Bankside. They moved there in 1599. Threatened by difficulties in renewing the lease on the land where their first playhouse (the Theatre) had been built, Shakespeare's company took advantage of the Christmas holiday in 1598 to dismantle the Theatre and transport its timbers across the Thames to the Bankside, where, in 1599, these timbers were used in the building of the Globe. The weather in late December 1598 is recorded as having been especially harsh. It was so cold that the Thames was "nigh [nearly] frozen," and there was heavy snow. Perhaps the weather aided Shakespeare's company in eluding their landlord, the snow hiding their activity and the freezing of the Thames allowing them to slide the timbers across to the Bankside without paying tolls for repeated trips over London Bridge. Attractive as this narrative is, it remains just as likely that the heavy snow hampered transport of the timbers in wagons through the London streets to the river. It also must be remembered that the Thames was, according to report, only "nigh frozen" and therefore as impassable as it ever was. Whatever the precise circumstances of this fascinating event in English theater history, Shakespeare's company was able to begin playing at their new Globe theater on the Bankside in 1599. After the first Globe burned down in 1613 during the staging of Shakespeare's *Henry VIII* (its thatch roof was set alight by cannon fire called for by the performance), Shakespeare's company immediately rebuilt on the same location. The second Globe seems to have been a grander structure than its predecessor. It remained in use until the beginning of the English Civil War in 1642, when Parliament officially closed the theaters. Soon thereafter it was pulled down.

The public theaters of Shakespeare's time were very different buildings from our theaters today. First of all, they were open-air playhouses. As recent excavations of the Rose and the Globe confirm, some were polygonal or roughly circular in shape; the Fortune, however, was square. The most recent estimates of their size put the diameter of these buildings at 72 feet (the Rose) to 100 feet (the Globe), but they were said to hold vast audiences of two or three thousand, who must have been squeezed together quite tightly. Some of these spectators paid extra to sit or stand in the two or three levels of roofed galleries that extended, on the upper levels, all the way around the theater and surrounded an open space. In this space were the stage and, perhaps, the tiring house (what we would call dressing rooms), as well as the so-called-yard. In the yard stood the spectators who chose to pay less, the ones whom Hamlet contemptuously called "groundlings." For a roof they had only the sky, and so they were exposed to all kinds of weather. They stood on a floor that was sometimes made of mortar and sometimes of ash mixed with the shells of hazelnuts. The latter provided a porous and therefore dry footing for the crowd, and the shells may have been more comfortable to stand on because they were not as hard as mortar. Availability of shells may not have been a problem if hazelnuts were a favorite food for Shakespeare's audiences to munch on as they watched his plays. Archaeologists who are today unearthing the remains of theaters from this period have discovered quantities of these nutshells on theater sites.

Unlike the yard, the stage itself was covered by a roof. Its ceiling, called "the heavens," is thought to have been elaborately painted to depict the sun, moon, stars, and planets. Just how big the stage was remains hard to determine. We have a single sketch of part of the interior of the Swan. A Dutchman named Johannes de Witt visited this theater around 1596 and sent a sketch of it back to his friend, Arend van Buchel. Because van Buchel found de Witt's letter and sketch of interest, he copied both into a book. It is van Buchel's copy, adapted, it seems, to the shape and size of the page in his book, that survives. In this sketch, the stage appears to be a large rectangular platform that thrusts far out into the yard, perhaps even as far as the center of the circle formed by the surrounding galleries. This drawing, combined with the specifications for the size of the stage in the building contract for the Fortune, has led scholars to conjecture that the stage on which Shakespeare's plays were performed must have measured approximately 43 feet in width and 27 feet in depth, a vast acting area. But the digging up of a large part of the Rose by archaeologists has provided evidence of a quite different stage design. The Rose stage was a platform tapered at the corners and much shallower than what seems to be depicted in the van Buchel sketch. Indeed, its measurements seem to be about 37.5 feet across at its widest point and only 15.5 feet deep. Because the surviving indications of stage size and design differ from each other so much, it is possible that the stages in other playhouses, like the Theatre, the Curtain, and the Globe (the outdoor playhouses where Shakespeare's plays were performed), were different from those at both the Swan and the Rose.

After about 1608 Shakespeare's plays were staged not only at the Globe but also at an indoor or private playhouse in Blackfriars. This theater had been constructed in 1596 by James Burbage in an upper hall of a former Dominican priory or monastic house. Although Henry VIII had dissolved all English monasteries in the 1530s (shortly after he had founded the Church of England), the area remained under church, rather than hostile civic, control. The hall that Burbage had purchased and renovated was a large one in which Parliament had once met. In the private theater that he constructed, the stage, lit by candles, was built across the narrow end of the hall, with boxes flanking it. The rest of the hall offered seating room only. Because there was no provision for standing room, the largest audience it could hold was less than a thousand, or about a quarter of what the Globe could accommodate. Admission to Blackfriars was correspondingly more expensive. Instead of a penny to stand in the yard at the Globe, it cost a minimum of sixpence to get into Blackfriars. The best seats at the Globe (in the Lords' Room in the gallery above and behind the stage) cost sixpence; but the boxes flanking the stage at Blackfriars were half a crown, or five times sixpence. Some spectators who were particularly interested in displaying themselves paid even more to sit on stools on the Blackfriars stage.

Whether in the outdoor or indoor playhouses, the stages of Shakespeare's time were different from ours. They were not separated from the audience by the dropping of a curtain between acts and scenes. Therefore the playwrights of the time had to find other ways of signaling to the audience that one scene (to be imagined as occurring in one location at a given time) had ended and the next (to be imagined at perhaps a different location at a later time) had begun. The customary way used by Shakespeare and many of his contemporaries was to have everyone onstage exit at the end of one scene and have one or more different characters enter to begin the next. In a few cases, where characters remain onstage from one scene to another, the dialogue or stage action makes the change of location clear, and the characters are generally to be imagined as having moved from one place to another. For example, in *Romeo and Juliet*, Romeo and his friends remain onstage in Act 1 from scene 4 to scene 5, but they are represented as having moved between scenes from the street that leads to Capulet's house into Capulet's house itself. The new location is signaled in part by the appearance onstage of Capulet's servingmen carrying napkins, something they would not take into the streets. Playwrights had to be quite resourceful in the use of hand properties, like the napkin, or in the use of dialogue to specify where the action was taking place in their plays because, in contrast to most of today's theaters, the playhouses of Shakespeare's time did not use movable scenery to dress the stage and make the setting precise. As another consequence of this difference, however, the playwrights of Shakespeare's time did not have to specify exactly where the action of their plays was set when they did not choose to do so, and much of the action of their plays is tied to no specific place.

Usually Shakespeare's stage is referred to as a "bare stage," to distinguish it from the stages of the last two or three centuries with their elaborate sets. But the stage in Shakespeare's time was not completely bare. Philip Henslowe, owner of the Rose, lists in his inventory of stage properties a rock, three tombs, and two mossy banks. Stage directions in plays of the time also call for such things as thrones (or "states"), banquets (presumably tables with plaster replicas of food on them), and beds and tombs to be pushed onto the stage. Thus the stage often held more than the actors.

The actors did not limit their performing to the stage alone. Occasionally they went beneath the stage, as the Ghost appears to do in the first act of *Hamlet*. From there they could emerge onto the stage through a trapdoor. They could retire behind the hangings across the back of the stage (or the front of the tiring house), as, for example, the actor playing Polonius does when he hides behind the arras. Sometimes the hangings could be drawn back during a performance to "discover" one or more actors behind them. When performance required that an actor appear "above," as when Juliet is imagined to stand at the window of her chamber in the famous and misnamed "balcony scene," then the actor probably climbed the stairs to the gallery over the back of the stage and temporarily shared it with some of the spectators. The stage was also provided with ropes and winches so that actors could descend from, and reascend to, the "heavens."

Perhaps the greatest difference between dramatic

performances in Shakespeare's time and ours was that in Shakespeare's England the roles of women were played by boys. (Some of these boys grew up to take male roles in their maturity.) There were no women in the acting companies, only in the audience. It had not always been so in the history of the English stage. There are records of women on English stages in the thirteenth and fourteenth centuries, two hundred years before Shakespeare's plays were performed. After the accession of James I in 1603, the queen of England and her ladies took part in entertainments at court called masques, and with the reopening of the theaters in 1660 at the restoration of Charles II, women again took their place on the public stage.

The chief competitors for the companies of adult actors such as the one to which Shakespeare belonged and for which he wrote were companies of exclusively boy actors. The competition was most intense in the early 1600s. There were then two principal children's companies: the Children of Paul's (the choirboys from St. Paul's Cathedral, whose private playhouse was near the cathedral); and the Children of the Chapel Royal (the choirboys from the monarch's private chapel, who performed at the Blackfriars theater built by Burbage in 1596, which Shakespeare's company had been stopped from using by local residents who objected to crowds). In *Hamlet* Shakespeare writes of "an aerie [nest] of children, little eyases [hawks], that cry out on the top of question and are most tyrannically clapped for 't. These are now the fashion and . . . berattle the common stages [attack the public theaters]." In the long run, the adult actors prevailed. The Children of Paul's dissolved around 1606. By about 1608 the Children of the Chapel Royal had been forced to stop playing at the Blackfriars theater, which was then taken over by the King's company of players, Shakespeare's own troupe.

Acting companies and theaters of Shakespeare's time were organized in different ways. For example, Philip Henslowe owned the Rose and leased it to companies of actors, who paid him from their takings. Henslowe would act as manager of these companies, initially paying playwrights for their plays and buying properties, recovering his outlay from the actors. With the building of the Globe, however, Shakespeare's company managed itself, with the principal actors, Shakespeare among them, having the status of "sharers" and the right to a share in the takings, as well as the responsibility for a part of the expenses. Five of the sharers, including Shakespeare, owned the Globe. As actor, as sharer in an acting company and in ownership of theaters, and as playwright, Shakespeare was about as involved in the theatrical industry as one could imagine. Although Shakespeare and his fellows prospered, their status under the law was conditional upon the protection of powerful patrons. "Common players"—those who did not have patrons or masters—were classed in the language of the law with "vagabonds and sturdy beggars." So the actors had to secure for themselves the official rank of servants of patrons. Among the patrons under whose protection Shakespeare's company worked were the lord chamberlain and, after the accession of King James in 1603, the king himself.

We are now perhaps on the verge of learning a great deal more about the theaters in which Shakespeare and his contemporaries performed—or at least of opening up new questions about them. Already about 70 percent of the Rose has been excavated, as has about 10 percent of the second Globe, the one built in 1614. It is to be hoped that soon more will be available for study. These are exciting times for students of Shakespeare's stage.

The Publication of
Shakespeare's Plays

Eighteen of Shakespeare's plays found their way into
print during the playwright's lifetime, but there is nothing to suggest that he took any interest in their publication. These eighteen appeared separately in editions
called quartos. Their pages were not much larger than
the one you are now reading, and these little books
were sold unbound for a few pence. The earliest of the
quartos that still survive were printed in 1594, the year
that both *Titus Andronicus* and a version of the play
now called *2 King Henry VI* became available. While
almost every one of these early quartos displays on its
title page the name of the acting company that performed the play, only about half provide the name of
the playwright, Shakespeare. The first quarto edition to
bear the name Shakespeare on its title page is *Love's
Labor's Lost* of 1598. A few of these quartos were popular with the book-buying public of Shakespeare's lifetime; for example, quarto *Richard II* went through five
editions between 1597 and 1615. But most of the quartos were far from best-sellers; *Love's Labor's Lost*
(1598), for instance, was not reprinted in quarto until
1631. After Shakespeare's death, two more of his plays
appeared in quarto format: *Othello* in 1622 and *The
Two Noble Kinsmen*, coauthored with John Fletcher, in
1634.

In 1623, seven years after Shakespeare's death, *Mr.
William Shakespeares Comedies, Histories, & Tragedies*
was published. This printing offered readers in a single book thirty-six of the thirty-eight plays now
thought to have been written by Shakespeare, includ-

ing eighteen that had never been printed before. And it offered them in a style that was then reserved for serious literature and scholarship. The plays were arranged in double columns on pages nearly a foot high. This large page size is called "folio," as opposed to the smaller "quarto," and the 1623 volume is usually called the Shakespeare First Folio. It is reputed to have sold for the lordly price of a pound. (One copy at the Folger Library is marked fifteen shillings—that is, three-quarters of a pound.)

In a preface to the First Folio entitled "To the great Variety of Readers," two of Shakespeare's former fellow actors in the King's Men, John Heminge and Henry Condell, wrote that they themselves had collected their dead companion's plays. They suggested that they had seen his own papers: "we have scarce received from him a blot in his papers." The title page of the Folio declared that the plays within it had been printed "according to the True Original Copies." Comparing the Folio to the quartos, Heminge and Condell disparaged the quartos, advising their readers that "before you were abused with divers stolen and surreptitious copies, maimed, and deformed by the frauds and stealths of injurious impostors." Many Shakespeareans of the eighteenth and nineteenth centuries believed Heminge and Condell and regarded the Folio plays as superior to anything in the quartos.

Once we begin to examine the Folio plays in detail, it becomes less easy to take at face value the word of Heminge and Condell about the superiority of the Folio texts. For example, of the first nine plays in the Folio (one-quarter of the entire collection), four were essentially reprinted from earlier quarto printings that Heminge and Condell had disparaged; and four have now been identified as printed from copies written in the hand of a professional scribe of the 1620s named Ralph Crane; the ninth, *The Comedy of Errors*, was apparently also printed from a manuscript, but one whose origin cannot be readily identified. Evidently then, eight of the first nine plays in the First Folio were not printed, in spite of what the Folio title page announces, "according to the True Original Copies," or Shakespeare's own papers, and the source of the ninth is unknown. Since today's editors have been forced to treat Heminge and Condell's pronouncements with skepticism, they must choose whether to base their own editions upon quartos or the Folio on grounds other than Heminge and Condell's story of where the quarto and Folio versions originated.

Editors have often fashioned their own narratives to explain what lies behind the quartos and Folio. They have said that Heminge and Condell meant to criticize only a few of the early quartos, the ones that offer much shorter and sometimes quite different, often garbled, versions of plays. Among the examples of these are the 1600 quarto of *Henry V* (the Folio offers a much fuller version) or the 1603 *Hamlet* quarto (in 1604 a different, much longer form of the play got into print as a quarto). Early-twentieth-century editors speculated that these questionable texts were produced when someone in the audience took notes from the plays' dialogue during performances and then employed "hack poets" to fill out the notes. The poor results were then sold to a publisher and presented in print as Shakespeare's plays. More recently this story has given way to another in which the shorter versions are said to be re-creations from memory of Shakespeare's plays by actors who wanted to stage them in the provinces but lacked manuscript copies. Most of the quartos offer much better texts than these so-called bad quartos. Indeed, in most of the quartos we find texts that are at least equal to or better than what is printed in the Folio. Many Shakespeare enthusiasts persuaded themselves that most of the quartos were set into type directly from Shakespeare's own papers, although there is nothing on which to base this conclusion except the desire for it to be true. Thus speculation continues about how the Shakespeare plays got to be printed. All that we have are the printed texts.

The book collector who was most successful in bringing together copies of the quartos and the First Folio was Henry Clay Folger, founder of the Folger Shakespeare Library in Washington, D.C. While it is estimated that there survive around the world only about 230 copies of the First Folio, Mr. Folger was able to acquire more than seventy-five copies, as well as a large number of fragments, for the library that bears his name. He also amassed a substantial number of quartos. For example, only fourteen copies of the First Quarto of *Love's Labor's Lost* are known to exist, and three are at the Folger Shakespeare Library. As a consequence of Mr. Folger's labors, scholars visiting the Folger Library have been able to learn a great deal about sixteenth- and seventeenth-century printing and, particularly, about the printing of Shakespeare's plays. And Mr. Folger did not stop at the First Folio, but collected many copies of later editions of Shakespeare, beginning with the Second Folio (1632), the Third (1663–64), and the Fourth (1685). Each of these later folios was based on its immediate predecessor and was edited anonymously. The first editor of Shakespeare whose name we know was Nicholas Rowe, whose first edition came out in 1709. Mr. Folger collected this edition and many, many more by Rowe's successors.

An Introduction to This Text

Titus Andronicus was first published in a quarto of 1594 (Q); this printing survives in only a single copy, now at the Folger Shakespeare Library. Q was reprinted in the Second Quarto (Q2) in 1600, which corrected a number of fairly obvious errors but also introduced many more. Evidently, the copy of Q used by the printer of Q2 had suffered damage at the bottom of its last two leaves, the damage resulting in the loss of several lines; the Q2 printer made up lines to take the place of these and added four lines to the end of the play. Until the single surviving copy of Q was found early in the twentieth century, the Q2 printer's lines were universally accepted as authentic. Q2 was reprinted in a Third Quarto (Q3) of 1611. When what we now call the Shakespeare First Folio was published in 1623, it contained a text of *Titus Andronicus* that in large part simply reprinted Q3. However, F also provided an additional scene, 3.2, the so-called fly scene, as well as a few readings, mainly in the stage directions, that seem to exceed the capacity of any printer to introduce. The additional scene demonstrates that the F printer had access to fresh manuscript copy. If the scene and the new readings elsewhere in the F version come from the same manuscript, then that manuscript may have been a theatrical one. This kind of manuscript would pay attention, as do the stage directions unique to F, to the sounds, the flourishes or trumpet blasts, that accompany performance.

This present edition is based on the Q printing of the

play* but also includes F's 3.2 (the "fly scene") and a number of F's new readings; the Folio material is placed within brackets, as described below. For the convenience of the reader, we have modernized the punctuation and the spelling of the Quarto and Folio material. Sometimes we go so far as to modernize certain old forms of words; for example, usually when *a* means *he*, we change it to *he*; we change *mo* to *more*, and *ye* to *you*. But it is not our practice in editing any of the plays to modernize words that sound distinctly different from modern forms. For example, when the early printed texts read *sith* or *apricocks* or *porpentine*, we have not modernized to *since, apricots, porcupine*. When the forms *an, and,* or *and if* appear instead of the modern form *if*, we have reduced *and* to *an* but have not changed any of these forms to their modern equivalent, *if*. We also modernize and, where necessary, correct passages in foreign languages, unless an error in the early printed text can be reasonably explained as a joke.

Whenever we change the wording of Q or, in 3.2, of F or add anything to Q's stage directions, we mark the change by enclosing it either in superior half-brackets (⌈ ⌉) or in pointed brackets (⟨ ⟩). If the change is one first found in F, we enclose it in pointed brackets; if the change originated in an edition without the authority lent to F by its reference to fresh manuscript copy— i.e., Q2 or Q3 or any edition later than F—we enclose it in square half-brackets. We employ these brackets because we want our readers to be immediately aware when we have intervened. (Only when we correct an obvious typographical error in Q or, in 3.2, in F does

---

*We have also consulted the computerized text of the First Quarto provided by the Text Archive of the Oxford University Computing Centre, to which we are grateful.

the change not get marked.) Whenever we change the wording of Q or, in 3.2, of F, or alter their punctuation so that meaning changes, we list the change in the textual notes at the back of the book, even if all we have done is fix an obvious error.

We regularize spellings of a number of the proper names, as is the usual practice in editions of the play. For example, Q sometimes calls Titus Andronicus's family "the Andronicy" or "the Andronicie," but we use the spelling "Andronici" throughout the text. We also expand the often severely abbreviated forms of names used as speech headings in early printed texts into the full names of the characters. We also regularize the speakers' names in speech headings, using only a single designation for each character, even though the early printed texts sometimes use a variety of designations. For example, in Q's speech prefixes, the Emperor Saturninus is sometimes called by his proper name, and sometimes called *"Emperour"* and sometimes *"King,"* but in this edition he is always called "Saturninus" in speech prefixes. Variations in the speech headings of the early printed texts are recorded in the textual notes.

This edition differs from many earlier ones in its efforts to aid the reader in imagining the play as a performance rather than as a series of actual events. In the play's first scene, for example, Titus makes clear that he brings back with him from his war with the Goths coffins containing the bodies of the sons he has lost in battle. In the same scene he also refers to his chariot. Some editors provide stage directions calling for multiple coffins (and multiple tombs in which to put them) as well as the chariot, the presence of which would seem to demand the addition of horses to draw it. Q, in contrast, calls for a single coffin and a single tomb, no chariot and no horses. We prefer not to add to Q directions that would require the stage, as it often came to be in the eighteenth and nineteenth centuries, to be filled with properties (coffins, a chariot drawn by horses) and a set (in the form of tombs) because we see no need to make performance represent every detail of the fiction. Instead we find it is more likely that performance both then and now present a symbolic version of the fiction. One coffin and one tomb stand for multiples of each; Titus's verbal reference to his chariot serves by itself to bring it to the stage and into the imagination of the audience.

Whenever it is reasonably certain, in our view, that a speech is accompanied by a particular action, we provide a stage direction describing the action, setting the added direction in brackets to signal that it is not found in Q or, in 3.2, in F. (Exceptions to this rule occur when the action is so obvious that to add a stage direction would insult the reader, and there are many such exceptions in *Titus Andronicus* since the dialogue itself is often so powerfully clear in its indications of actions—actions often so horrific that there is nothing to be gained by repeating them in additional stage directions.) Stage directions for the entrance of a character in mid-scene are, with rare exceptions, placed so that they immediately precede the character's participation in the scene, even though these entrances may appear somewhat earlier in the early printed texts. Whenever we move a stage direction, we record this change in the textual notes. Latin stage directions (e.g., *Exeunt*) are translated into English (e.g., *They exit*).

In the present edition, as well, we mark with a dash any change of address within a speech, unless a stage direction intervenes. When the -ed ending of a word is to be pronounced, we mark it with an accent. Like editors for the past two centuries, we print metrically linked lines in the following way:

BASSIANUS
  Lavinia, how say you?
LAVINIA   I say no.

(2.2.16–17)

However, when there are a number of short verse-lines that can be linked in more than one way, we do not, with rare exceptions, indent any of them.

The Explanatory Notes

The notes that appear on the pages facing the text are designed to provide readers with the help that they may need to enjoy the play. Whenever the meaning of a word in the text is not readily accessible in a good contemporary dictionary, we offer the meaning in a note. Sometimes we provide a note even when the relevant meaning is to be found in the dictionary but when the word has acquired since Shakespeare's time other potentially confusing meanings. In our notes, we try to offer modern synonyms for Shakespeare's words. We also try to indicate to the reader the connection between the word in the play and the modern synonym. For example, Shakespeare sometimes uses the word *head* to mean *source*, but, for modern readers, there may be no connection evident between these two words. We provide the connection by explaining Shakespeare's usage as follows: "**head:** fountainhead, source." On some occasions, a whole phrase or clause needs explanation. Then we rephrase in our own words the difficult passage, and add at the end synonyms for individual words in the passage. When scholars have been unable to determine the meaning of a word or phrase, we acknowledge the uncertainty. Whenever we provide a passage from the Bible to illuminate the text of the play, we use the Geneva Bible of 1560 (with spelling modernized).

TITUS
ANDRONICUS

Characters in the Play

TITUS ANDRONICUS, a noble Roman general
LAVINIA, his daughter
LUCIUS
MUTIUS
MARTIUS } *his sons*
QUINTUS
YOUNG LUCIUS, his grandson

MARCUS ANDRONICUS, Titus's brother, a Roman tribune
PUBLIUS, his son

SEMPRONIUS
CAIUS } *Titus's kinsmen*
VALENTINE

SATURNINUS, elder son of the former Roman emperor, later
    emperor
BASSIANUS, younger son of the former emperor

TAMORA, Queen of the Goths, later empress
AARON the Moor, Tamora's lover
ALARBUS
DEMETRIUS } *Tamora's sons*
CHIRON

AEMILIUS, a Roman nobleman

MESSENGER
NURSE
A Roman CAPTAIN
COUNTRY FELLOW
FIRST GOTH
SECOND GOTH

Tribunes, Senators, Romans, Goths, Drummers,
Trumpeters, Soldiers, Guards, Attendants, a black Child

3

TITUS
ANDRONICUS

ACT 1

1.1.1–235 Saturninus and Bassianus, sons of the deceased Emperor of Rome, challenge each other for the title of emperor. Titus Andronicus, general of the Roman forces, enters with captives from the recent war, along with his remaining sons, some living, some dead. Titus allows the eldest son of the captive Queen of the Goths to be slain in retribution for his own sons' deaths. Titus is then asked by his brother, the tribune Marcus, to stand as a candidate for Emperor of Rome. Instead, Titus names Saturninus as emperor.

(continued)

----

0 SD. **Flourish:** a horn fanfare to announce the arrival of important persons; **Tribunes:** officials appointed to protect the common people or plebeians against the patricians, represented by the **Senators; Drums and Trumpets:** i.e., drummers and trumpeters

4. **Plead:** maintain; **successive:** hereditary

5–6. **his firstborn . . . Rome:** i.e., eldest **son** of the last emperor

8. **Nor:** i.e., do not; **mine age:** i.e., my status as eldest; **this indignity:** i.e., being challenged by a younger brother

10. **Caesar's son:** i.e., the son of an emperor

11. **Were gracious:** found acceptance

12. **Keep:** guard, defend; **Capitol:** Temple of Jupiter Capitolinus on the Capitoline Hill, mistakenly identified with the Senate House, which was actually located at the foot of the Hill (See Shakespeare's *Julius Caesar* 2.4.1 and 13, and 63 SD, below.)

(continued)

⟨ACT 1⟩

⟨Scene 1⟩

⟨*Flourish.*⟩ *Enter the Tribunes (⌐including Marcus An-*
dronicus⌐) and Senators aloft. And then enter, ⌐below,⌐
Saturninus and his followers at one door, and
Bassianus and his followers ⌐at another door,⌐ with
⌐other Romans,⌐ Drums, and Trumpets.

SATURNINUS
  Noble patricians, patrons of my right,
  Defend the justice of my cause with arms.
  And countrymen, my loving followers,
  Plead my successive title with your swords.
  I am his firstborn son that was the last   5
  That wore the imperial diadem of Rome.
  Then let my father's honors live in me,
  Nor wrong mine age with this indignity.
BASSIANUS
  Romans, friends, followers, favorers of my right,
  If ever Bassianus, Caesar's son,   10
  Were gracious in the eyes of royal Rome,
  Keep, then, this passage to the Capitol,
  And suffer not dishonor to approach
  The imperial seat, to virtue consecrate,
  To justice, continence, and nobility;   15
  But let desert in pure election shine,
  And, Romans, fight for freedom in your choice.

13. **suffer:** allow

14–15. **to virtue . . . justice:** dedicated **to virtue, to justice**

15. **continence:** self-restraint

16. **pure election:** unconditional choice

19. **empery:** emperorship

20–21. **for whom . . . special party:** i.e., whose particular interest we represent

23. **surnamèd:** called (because of his character); **Pius:** patriotic, dutiful, religious, just

24. **deserts:** meritorious actions

27. **accited:** summoned

28. **barbarous:** (1) savage; (2) non-Latin-speaking; **Goths:** members of a Germanic tribe that became powerful during the later Roman Empire

30. **yoked:** subjugated

35. **field:** At this point in the 1594 Quarto are found three and a half lines that are inconsistent with the order of the action as presented in the rest of this scene. They may be found in the Textual Notes, page 216.

38. **flourishing:** eminent, conspicuous

39–40. **by honor . . . succeed:** i.e., in the name of the candidate whom you prefer

42. **Whom:** i.e., which (with reference to **the Capitol and Senate's right**); **pretend:** claim

43. **withdraw you:** i.e., **withdraw**

44. **suitors:** petitioners

46. **fair:** courteously, suitably

47. **affy:** put my trust

MARCUS, (⟨*aloft,*⟩ ⌜*stepping forward and holding up*⌝ *the crown*)

  Princes that strive by factions and by friends
  Ambitiously for rule and empery,
  Know that the people of Rome, for whom we stand   20
  A special party, have by common voice,
  In election for the Roman empery,
  Chosen Andronicus, surnamèd Pius
  For many good and great deserts to Rome.
  A nobler man, a braver warrior,   25
  Lives not this day within the city walls.
  He by the Senate is accited home
  From weary wars against the barbarous Goths,
  That with his sons, a terror to our foes,
  Hath yoked a nation strong, trained up in arms.   30
  Ten years are spent since first he undertook
  This cause of Rome, and chastisèd with arms
  Our enemies' pride. Five times he hath returned
  Bleeding to Rome, bearing his valiant sons
  In coffins from the field.   35
  And now at last, laden with honor's spoils,
  Returns the good Andronicus to Rome,
  Renownèd Titus flourishing in arms.
  Let us entreat, by honor of his name
  Whom worthily you would have now succeed,   40
  And in the Capitol and Senate's right,
  Whom you pretend to honor and adore,
  That you withdraw you and abate your strength,
  Dismiss your followers and, as suitors should,
  Plead your deserts in peace and humbleness.   45

SATURNINUS
  How fair the tribune speaks to calm my thoughts!

BASSIANUS
  Marcus Andronicus, so I do affy
  In thy uprightness and integrity,

51. **all:** entirely

55. **in balance:** i.e., as if in a balance scale (See picture, page 40.)

61. **confident:** trustful

63. **poor competitor:** rival of humble station (as the younger brother)

69. **to yoke:** i.e., into submission (See longer note, page 209.)

69 SD 3, 7. **coffin:** See longer note, page 209.

"Sound . . . trumpets." (1.1.69 SD, 149 SD)
From Guillaume Du Choul, *Los discursos de la religion . . .* (1579).

And so I love and honor thee and thine,
Thy noble brother Titus and his sons,   50
And her to whom my thoughts are humbled all,
Gracious Lavinia, Rome's rich ornament,
That I will here dismiss my loving friends,
And to my fortunes and the people's favor
Commit my cause in balance to be weighed.   55
                         ⌜*Bassianus'*⌝ *Soldiers exit.*

SATURNINUS
    Friends that have been thus forward in my right,
    I thank you all and here dismiss you all,
    And to the love and favor of my country
    Commit myself, my person, and the cause.
                         ⌜*Saturninus' Soldiers exit.*⌝
    Rome, be as just and gracious unto me   60
    As I am confident and kind to thee.
    Open the gates and let me in.

BASSIANUS
    Tribunes, and me, a poor competitor.
    ⟨*Flourish.*⟩ *They* ⌜*exit to*⌝ *go up into the Senate House.*
    ⌜*The Tribunes and Senators exit from the upper stage.*⌝

                    Enter a Captain.

⟨CAPTAIN⟩
    Romans, make way! The good Andronicus,
    Patron of virtue, Rome's best champion,   65
    Successful in the battles that he fights,
    With honor and with fortune is returned
    From where he circumscrìbed with his sword
    And brought to yoke the enemies of Rome.

Sound drums and trumpets, and then enter two of Titus'
sons (⌜*Lucius and Mutius*⌝*) and then two men bearing a*
coffin covered with black, then two other sons (⌜*Martius*
and Quintus⌝*), then Titus Andronicus, and then Tamora*
the Queen of Goths and her sons ⌜*Alarbus,*⌝ *Chiron and*

70. **weeds:** garments

71. **bark:** ship; **discharged:** unloaded; **his:** i.e., its; **fraught:** freight

72. **lading:** cargo

73. **she weighed her anchorage:** i.e., it raised its anchors

74. **bound with laurel boughs:** i.e., his head wreathed in **laurel** to signal his victory (See picture, page 18.)

77. **Thou . . . Capitol:** Jupiter, or Jove, king of the Roman gods (For **Capitol,** see note to line 12, above, and picture, page 14.)

78. **Stand:** be

80. **Priam:** legendary king of Troy, who had fifty sons and many daughters (See picture, page 122.)

81. **remains:** remaining part

83. **latest:** final

85. **given me leave:** permitted me (an ironic way to describe their defeat)

86. **unkind:** unnatural; undutiful

88. **Styx:** in classical mythology, a river in the underworld across which the souls of the dead had to cross (Until the body was properly buried, the soul could not cross to find peace.)

94. **in store:** i.e., in your keeping

96. **proudest:** highest-ranking

98. **Ad manes fratrum:** to the spirits of [our] brothers (Latin)

100. **shadows:** disembodied spirits, ghosts

101. **prodigies:** unnatural happenings, marvels

Demetrius, with Aaron the Moor, and others as many as
can be, then set down the coffin, and Titus speaks.

TITUS

    Hail Rome, victorious in thy mourning weeds!   70
    Lo, as the bark that hath discharged his fraught
    Returns with precious lading to the bay
    From whence at first she weighed her anchorage,
    Cometh Andronicus, bound with laurel boughs,
    To resalute his country with his tears,   75
    Tears of true joy for his return to Rome.
    Thou great defender of this Capitol,
    Stand gracious to the rites that we intend.
    Romans, of five-and-twenty valiant sons,
    Half of the number that King Priam had,   80
    Behold the poor remains alive and dead.
    These that survive let Rome reward with love;
    These that I bring unto their latest home,
    With burial amongst their ancestors.
    Here Goths have given me leave to sheathe my sword.   85
    Titus, unkind and careless of thine own,
    Why suffer'st thou thy sons unburied yet
    To hover on the dreadful shore of Styx?
    Make way to lay them by their brethren.
                              They open the tomb.
    There greet in silence, as the dead are wont,   90
    And sleep in peace, slain in your country's wars.
    O sacred receptacle of my joys,
    Sweet cell of virtue and nobility,
    How many sons hast thou of mine in store
    That thou wilt never render to me more?   95

LUCIUS

    Give us the proudest prisoner of the Goths,
    That we may hew his limbs and on a pile,
    Ad manes fratrum, sacrifice his flesh
    Before this earthy prison of their bones,
    That so the shadows be not unappeased,   100
    Nor we disturbed with prodigies on earth.

106. **passion:** grief
109. **Sufficeth not:** i.e., does it **not** suffice
110. **triumphs:** A *triumph* was the entrance of a victorious commander with his army, spoils, and captives in procession into Rome.
114. **commonweal:** commonwealth, state
116. **tomb:** i.e., family **tomb**
121. **Patient:** calm, quiet
122. **their:** i.e., my sons'
127. **straight:** straightaway, immediately
129. **clean:** entirely

CAPITOLIVM

The Capitol. (1.1.41, 77)
From Giacomo Lauri, *Antiquae vrbis splendor . . .* (1612–15).

TITUS

I give him you, the noblest that survives,
The eldest son of this distressèd queen.

TAMORA

Stay, Roman brethren!—Gracious conqueror,
Victorious Titus, rue the tears I shed,   105
A mother's tears in passion for her son.
And if thy sons were ever dear to thee,
O think my son to be as dear to me.
Sufficeth not that we are brought to Rome
To beautify thy triumphs and return   110
Captive to thee and to thy Roman yoke,
But must my sons be slaughtered in the streets
For valiant doings in their country's cause?
O, if to fight for king and commonweal
Were piety in thine, it is in these!   115

⌜*She kneels.*⌝

Andronicus, stain not thy tomb with blood.
Wilt thou draw near the nature of the gods?
Draw near them then in being merciful.
Sweet mercy is nobility's true badge.
Thrice-noble Titus, spare my first-born son.   120

TITUS

Patient yourself, madam, and pardon me.
These are their brethren whom your Goths beheld
Alive and dead, and for their brethren slain
Religiously they ask a sacrifice.
To this your son is marked, and die he must,   125
T' appease their groaning shadows that are gone.

LUCIUS

Away with him, and make a fire straight,
And with our swords upon a pile of wood
Let's hew his limbs till they be clean consumed.

Exit Titus' sons with Alarbus.

131. **Scythia:** ancient region in Eurasia whose people were noted in classical literature for their savagery (See picture, page 28.)

132. **Oppose . . . to:** contrast . . . with

135. **withal:** nevertheless; in addition

136–38. **Queen of Troy . . . Thracian tyrant:** Hecuba, wife of King Priam **of Troy,** avenged the murder of her son Polydorus by blinding his murderer, **the Thracian tyrant** Polymnestor. (See picture below.)

138. **in his tent:** See longer note, page 209.

141. **quit:** requite, repay

147. **larums:** trumpet blasts (that usually function as calls to arms)

149. **latest:** last

152. **chances:** i.e., mischances

153. **envy:** malice

154. **drugs:** i.e., plants from which poisonous **drugs** are made

Hecuba, Queen of Troy. (1.1.136; 4.1.20)
From [Guillaume Rouillé,] . . . *Promptuarii iconum* . . . (1553).

TAMORA, ⌜*rising and speaking aside to her sons*⌝
  O cruel, irreligious piety!   130
CHIRON, ⌜*aside to Tamora and Demetrius*⌝
  Was never Scythia half so barbarous!
DEMETRIUS, ⌜*aside to Tamora and Chiron*⌝
  Oppose not Scythia to ambitious Rome!
  Alarbus goes to rest and we survive
  To tremble under Titus' threat'ning look.
  Then, madam, stand resolved, but hope withal   135
  The selfsame gods that armed the Queen of Troy
  With opportunity of sharp revenge
  Upon the Thracian tyrant in his tent
  May favor Tamora the Queen of Goths
  (When Goths were Goths, and Tamora was queen)   140
  To quit the bloody wrongs upon her foes.

Enter the sons of Andronicus again ⌜*with bloody swords.*⌝

LUCIUS
  See, lord and father, how we have performed
  Our Roman rites. Alarbus' limbs are lopped,
  And entrails feed the sacrificing fire,
  Whose smoke like incense doth perfume the sky.   145
  Remaineth naught but to inter our brethren,
  And with loud larums welcome them to Rome.
TITUS
  Let it be so. And let Andronicus
  Make this his latest farewell to their souls.
      Sound trumpets, and lay the coffin in the tomb.
  In peace and honor rest you here, my sons,   150
  Rome's readiest champions, repose you here in rest,
  Secure from worldly chances and mishaps.
  Here lurks no treason, here no envy swells,
  Here grow no damnèd drugs; here are no storms,
  No noise, but silence and eternal sleep.   155
  In peace and honor rest you here, my sons.

Enter Lavinia.

159. **tributary tears: tears** offered as tribute

165. **reserved:** kept in store

166. **cordial of:** i.e., comfort to (Literally, a **cordial** is a drink.)

168. **date:** duration; **for:** i.e., as the object of

170. **triumpher:** conqueror; one celebrated in a triumph (See note to line 110 above.)

177. **That:** who; **Solon's happiness:** Solon, the fifth-century B.C.E. Athenian lawgiver, when asked who is happiest, said "Call no man happy until he is dead."

178. **honor's bed:** i.e., an honorable grave

181. **trust:** i.e., the one whom they trust

182. **palliament:** robe, gown

A laurel wreath of victory. (1.1.74)
From Giacomo Lauri, *Antiquae vrbis splendor* . . . (1612–15).

⌜LAVINIA⌝
    In peace and honor live Lord Titus long;
    My noble lord and father, live in fame.
                                    ⌜*She kneels.*⌝

    Lo, at this tomb my tributary tears
    I render for my brethren's obsequies,   160
    And at thy feet I kneel, with tears of joy
    Shed on this earth for thy return to Rome.
    O bless me here with thy victorious hand,
    Whose fortunes Rome's best citizens applaud.
TITUS
    Kind Rome, that hast thus lovingly reserved   165
    The cordial of mine age to glad my heart!—
    Lavinia, live, outlive thy father's days
    And fame's eternal date, for virtue's praise.
                                    ⌜*Lavinia rises.*⌝

    ⌜*Enter Marcus Andronicus, carrying a white robe.*
    Enter aloft Saturninus, Bassianus, Tribunes, Senators,
                    and Guards.⌝

MARCUS
    Long live Lord Titus, my belovèd brother,
    Gracious triumpher in the eyes of Rome.   170
TITUS
    Thanks, gentle tribune, noble brother Marcus.
MARCUS
    And welcome, nephews, from successful wars—
    You that survive, and you that sleep in fame.
    Fair lords, your fortunes are alike in all,
    That in your country's service drew your swords;   175
    But safer triumph is this funeral pomp,
    That hath aspired to Solon's happiness,
    And triumphs over chance in honor's bed.—
    Titus Andronicus, the people of Rome,
    Whose friend in justice thou hast ever been,   180
    Send thee by me, their tribune and their trust,
    This palliament of white and spotless hue,

183. **name thee in election:** i.e., nominate you; **empire:** emperorship

184. **With:** i.e., along with

185. **candidatus:** candidate (literally, "dressed in white" [Latin])

189. **What:** an interjection introducing a question

193. **set abroad:** perhaps, **set** abroach, **set** afoot

197. **Knighted in field:** an anachronistic allusion to the practice, not originating until the Middle Ages, of rewarding valor with knighthoods conferred on the battlefield

198. **right and service:** i.e., the **service** of the rightful cause

202. **obtain and ask: obtain** by merely asking

203. **canst thou tell:** perhaps a version of "when, can you tell," a colloquial way of denying someone's assertion

213. **wean them from themselves:** i.e., detach them from their desire (to elect me); reconcile them to the loss of their desires

And name thee in election for the empire
With these our late deceasèd emperor's sons.
Be *candidatus*, then, and put it on   185
And help to set a head on headless Rome.

TITUS
A better head her glorious body fits
Than his that shakes for age and feebleness.
⌜*To Tribunes and Senators aloft.*⌝ What, should I don
    this robe and trouble you?   190
Be chosen with proclamations today,
Tomorrow yield up rule, resign my life,
And set abroad new business for you all?
Rome, I have been thy soldier forty years,
And led my country's strength successfully,   195
And buried one and twenty valiant sons,
Knighted in field, slain manfully in arms,
In right and service of their noble country.
Give me a staff of honor for mine age,
But not a scepter to control the world.   200
Upright he held it, lords, that held it last.

MARCUS
Titus, thou shalt obtain and ask the empery.

SATURNINUS
Proud and ambitious tribune, canst thou tell?

TITUS   Patience, Prince Saturninus.

SATURNINUS   Romans, do me right.   205
Patricians, draw your swords and sheathe them not
Till Saturninus be Rome's emperor.—
Andronicus, would thou were shipped to hell
Rather than rob me of the people's hearts.

LUCIUS
Proud Saturnine, interrupter of the good   210
That noble-minded Titus means to thee.

TITUS
Content thee, prince. I will restore to thee
The people's hearts and wean them from themselves.

218. **meed:** reward
220. **voices, suffrages:** votes
223. **gratulate:** express joy at; greet
224. **admits:** i.e., accepts, acknowledges
225. **suit:** petition
228. **Titan's:** the sun's (In Roman mythology, Titan was the brother of Saturn and ancestor of the Titans. His name is used in poetry for the personified sun.)

1.1.236–347 Saturninus's first act as emperor is to choose Titus's daughter Lavinia as his bride. Titus willingly agrees. Bassianus claims that she is his own betrothed, and Titus's sons and his brother Marcus help Bassianus carry her away. Titus is enraged and kills his son Mutius, who is abetting their escape. Saturninus turns against Titus because of his family's actions and replaces Lavinia with Tamora, Queen of the Goths, as his bride, exiting to marry her immediately.

(continued)

———

238. **in part:** i.e., as **part**
239. **gentleness:** nobleness
240. **an onset:** a beginning

BASSIANUS
   Andronicus, I do not flatter thee,
   But honor thee, and will do till I die.   215
   My faction if thou strengthen with thy friends,
   I will most thankful be, and thanks, to men
   Of noble minds, is honorable meed.

TITUS
   People of Rome, and people's tribunes here,
   I ask your voices and your suffrages.   220
   Will you bestow them friendly on Andronicus?

TRIBUNES
   To gratify the good Andronicus
   And gratulate his safe return to Rome,
   The people will accept whom he admits.

TITUS
   Tribunes, I thank you, and this suit I make: 225
   That you create our emperor's eldest son,
   Lord Saturnine, whose virtues will, I hope,
   Reflect on Rome as ⌜Titan's⌝ rays on earth
   And ripen justice in this commonweal.
   Then, if you will elect by my advice,   230
   Crown him and say "Long live our emperor."

MARCUS
   With voices and applause of every sort,
   Patricians and plebeians, we create
   Lord Saturninus Rome's great emperor,
   And say "Long live our Emperor Saturnine."   235
        ⟨*A long flourish till* ⌜*Saturninus, Bassianus,*
                  and Guards⌝ *come down.*⟩

SATURNINUS
   Titus Andronicus, for thy favors done
   To us in our election this day,
   I give thee thanks in part of thy deserts,
   And will with deeds requite thy gentleness.
   And for an onset, Titus, to advance   240

244. **Pantheon:** temple consecrated to all the gods (See picture below.) **espouse:** marry
245. **motion:** proposal, suggestion
247. **honored of:** i.e., **honored** by
252. **imperious:** imperial
254. **ensigns:** tokens, signs
258. **unspeakable:** indescribable
261. **state:** high rank
263. **goodly:** beautiful
267. **cheer:** expression
268. **scorn:** object of mockery or contempt
271. **he comforts:** i.e., **he** who **comforts**

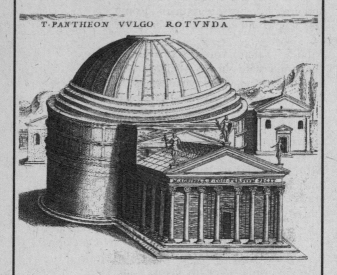

T·PANTHEON VVLGO ROTVNDA

The "sacred Pantheon." (1.1.244)
From Giacomo Lauri, *Antiquae vrbis splendor* . . . (1612–15).

Thy name and honorable family,
Lavinia will I make my empress,
Rome's royal mistress, mistress of my heart,
And in the sacred ⌜Pantheon⌝ her espouse.
Tell me, Andronicus, doth this motion please thee?   245

TITUS
It doth, my worthy lord, and in this match
I hold me highly honored of your Grace;
And here in sight of Rome to Saturnine,
King and commander of our commonweal,
The wide world's emperor, do I consecrate   250
My sword, my chariot, and my prisoners,
Presents well worthy Rome's imperious lord.
Receive them, then, the tribute that I owe,
Mine honor's ensigns humbled at thy feet.

SATURNINUS
Thanks, noble Titus, father of my life.   255
How proud I am of thee and of thy gifts
Rome shall record.—And when I do forget
The least of these unspeakable deserts,
Romans, forget your fealty to me.

TITUS, ⌜*to Tamora*⌝
Now, madam, are you prisoner to an emperor,   260
To him that for your honor and your state
Will use you nobly, and your followers.

SATURNINUS, ⌜*aside*⌝
A goodly lady, trust me, of the hue
That I would choose, were I to choose anew.—
Clear up, fair queen, that cloudy countenance.   265
Though ⌜chance⌝ of war hath wrought this change
    of cheer,
Thou com'st not to be made a scorn in Rome.
Princely shall be thy usage every way.
Rest on my word, and let not discontent   270
Daunt all your hopes. Madam, he comforts you
Can make you greater than the Queen of Goths.—
Lavinia, you are not displeased with this?

274. **sith:** since
275. **Warrants:** authorizes, sanctions
278. **trump:** trumpet
279. **maid:** maiden, unmarried young woman (Lavinia)
281. **withal:** as well, besides
282. **reason:** justice
283. **Suum cuique:** to each his own (Latin)
284. **seizeth:** puts himself in legal possession of
286. **avaunt:** be gone
287. **surprised:** taken, captured

LAVINIA
  Not I, my lord, sith true nobility
  Warrants these words in princely courtesy.   275

SATURNINUS
  Thanks, sweet Lavinia.—Romans, let us go.
  Ransomless here we set our prisoners free.
  Proclaim our honors, lords, with trump and drum.
⌜*Flourish. Saturninus and his Guards exit, with Drums
      and Trumpets. Tribunes and Senators exit aloft.*⌝

BASSIANUS
  Lord Titus, by your leave, this maid is mine.

TITUS
  How, sir? Are you in earnest then, my lord?   280

BASSIANUS
  Ay, noble Titus, and resolved withal
  To do myself this reason and this right.
            ⌜*Bassianus takes Lavinia by the arm.*⌝

MARCUS
  Suum ⌜*cuique*⌝ is our Roman justice.
  This prince in justice seizeth but his own.

LUCIUS
  And that he will and shall, if Lucius live!   285

TITUS
  Traitors, avaunt! Where is the Emperor's guard?

     ⌜*Enter Saturninus and his Guards.*⌝

  Treason, my lord. Lavinia is surprised.

SATURNINUS
  Surprised? By whom?

BASSIANUS   By him that justly may
  Bear his betrothed from all the world away.   290

MUTIUS
  Brothers, help to convey her hence away,
  And with my sword I'll keep this door safe.
          ⌜*Bassianus, Lavinia, Marcus, Lucius,
              Quintus, and Martius exit.*⌝

300. **Nor . . . nor:** i.e., neither . . . nor
303. **will:** wish
304. **That:** who
307. **by leisure:** barely; not at all
310. **Was none:** i.e., **was** there no one; **stale:** i.e., figure of ridicule (as a discarded lover)

The barbarous Scythian. (1.1.131)
From Conrad Lycosthenes, *Prodigiorum* . . . (1557).

TITUS, ⌐*to Saturninus*⌐
  Follow, my lord, and I'll soon bring her back.
                    ⌐*Saturninus, Tamora, Demetrius, Chiron,*
                        Aaron, and Guards exit.⌐
MUTIUS My lord, you pass not here.
TITUS   What, villain boy,   295
  Barr'st me my way in Rome?
                              ⌐*He stabs Mutius.*⌐
MUTIUS   Help, Lucius, help!
                              ⌐*Mutius dies.*⌐

                    ⌐*Enter Lucius.*⌐

LUCIUS
  My lord, you are unjust, and more than so!
  In wrongful quarrel you have slain your son.
TITUS
  Nor thou nor he are any sons of mine.   300
  My sons would never so dishonor me.
  Traitor, restore Lavinia to the Emperor.

  Enter aloft the Emperor ⌐*Saturninus*⌐ *with Tamora*
      and her two sons and Aaron the Moor.

LUCIUS
  Dead if you will, but not to be his wife
  That is another's lawful promised love.   ⌐*He exits.*⌐
SATURNINUS
  No, Titus, no, the Emperor needs her not,   305
  Nor her, nor thee, nor any of thy stock.
  I'll trust by leisure him that mocks me once,
  Thee never, nor thy traitorous haughty sons,
  Confederates all thus to dishonor me.
  Was none in Rome to make a stale   310
  But Saturnine? Full well, Andronicus,
  Agree these deeds with that proud brag of thine
  That said'st I begged the empire at thy hands.

315. **go thy ways:** a dismissive phrase; **changing piece:** faithless woman

316. **flourished . . . sword:** i.e., brandished **his sword for her**

318. **bandy:** contend, fight

319. **ruffle:** swagger

322. **Phoebe:** Diana, goddess of chastity, the moon, and the hunt; **nymphs:** demi-goddesses attendant on Diana, whose beauty "overshines" theirs (See picture, page 36.)

323. **gallant'st:** most gorgeous

326. **Emperess:** This Quarto spelling is retained for the sake of the meter.

327. **applaud:** approve of, agree to

330. **priest and holy water:** one of the play's many 'anachronistic references to the Roman Catholic Church (The play is set in pre-Christian times.)

332. **Hymenaeus:** Roman god of marriage (See picture below.) **stand:** i.e., stands

334. **climb:** i.e., go up to

Hymen, god of marriage. (1.1.332)
From Vincenzo Cartari, *Imagines deorum* . . . (1581).

TITUS
  O monstrous! What reproachful words are these?

SATURNINUS
  But go thy ways. Go give that changing piece   315
  To him that flourished for her with his sword.
  A valiant son-in-law thou shalt enjoy,
  One fit to bandy with thy lawless sons,
  To ruffle in the commonwealth of Rome.

TITUS
  These words are razors to my wounded heart.   320

SATURNINUS
  And therefore, lovely Tamora, Queen of Goths,
  That like the stately ⌜Phoebe⌝ 'mongst her nymphs
  Dost overshine the gallant'st dames of Rome,
  If thou be pleased with this my sudden choice,
  Behold, I choose thee, Tamora, for my bride,   325
  And will create thee Emperess of Rome.
  Speak, Queen of Goths, dost thou applaud my
     choice?
  And here I swear by all the Roman gods,
  Sith priest and holy water are so near,   330
  And tapers burn so bright, and everything
  In readiness for Hymenaeus stand,
  I will not resalute the streets of Rome
  Or climb my palace till from forth this place
  I lead espoused my bride along with me.   335

TAMORA
  And here in sight of heaven to Rome I swear,
  If Saturnine advance the Queen of Goths,
  She will a handmaid be to his desires,
  A loving nurse, a mother to his youth.

SATURNINUS
  Ascend, fair queen, ⌜to Pantheon.⌝—Lords, accompany   340
  Your noble emperor and his lovely bride,
  Sent by the heavens for Prince Saturnine,

343. **Whose ... conquerèd:** perhaps, Tamora's **wisdom** (in accepting Saturninus) has reversed **her** (bad) **fortune**

344. **consummate:** complete

345. **bid:** invited

347. **challengèd:** accused

1.1.348–505 Titus is persuaded by his family to allow the body of Mutius to be placed in the family tomb. Saturninus returns with his new empress, Tamora, and Bassianus and Lavinia, now married, enter with Titus's family. Tamora publicly urges Saturninus to forgive Bassianus, Titus, and his family. Speaking privately to Saturninus, she explains that this forgiveness is only for show: soon she will destroy all of them in revenge for the ritual sacrifice of her own son. Titus and the others believe they are forgiven, and Titus invites the Emperor and Empress to a hunt.

---

351. **confederates:** accomplices

354. **becomes:** is appropriate or fitting

358. **reedified:** restored; rebuilt

359. **servitors:** servants; soldiers; officials

Whose wisdom hath her fortune conquerèd.
There shall we consummate our spousal rites.

All ⌐but Titus¬ exit.

TITUS
I am not bid to wait upon this bride.   345
Titus, when wert thou wont to walk alone,
Dishonored thus and challengèd of wrongs?

*Enter Marcus and Titus' sons ⌐Lucius, Martius,
and Quintus.¬*

MARCUS
O Titus, see! O, see what thou hast done!
In a bad quarrel slain a virtuous son.
TITUS
No, foolish tribune, no; no son of mine,   350
Nor thou, nor these confederates in the deed
That hath dishonored all our family.
Unworthy brother and unworthy sons!
LUCIUS
But let us give him burial as becomes,
Give Mutius burial with our brethren.   355
TITUS
Traitors, away! He rests not in this tomb.
This monument five hundred years hath stood,
Which I have sumptuously reedified.
Here none but soldiers and Rome's servitors
Repose in fame, none basely slain in brawls.   360
Bury him where you can. He comes not here.
MARCUS
My lord, this is impiety in you.
My nephew Mutius' deeds do plead for him.
He must be buried with his brethren.
⌐MARTIUS¬
And shall, or him we will accompany.   365
TITUS
"And shall"? What villain was it spake that word?

367. **vouch it:** make it good

368. **in my despite:** in contemptuous defiance of me

371. **crest:** figure or device borne by a knight on his helmet (in a period long after the setting of this play) See picture, page 38.

375. **not with:** i.e., beside

379. **if . . . speed:** an obscure clause (**Speed** means "succeed.")

382. **Suffer:** allow

386. **advice:** deliberation; **Ajax:** a Greek hero in the Trojan War who, enraged at the Greek generals, in an insane fit slaughtered sheep he believed to be the generals, and then, recovering from his fit, **slew himself**

387. **Laertes' son:** Odysseus (in Latin, Ulysses), King of Ithaca in Greece (See picture below.)

388. **his funerals:** i.e., Ajax's funeral

Ulysses. (1.1.387)
From [Guillaume Rouillé,] . . . *Promptuarii iconum* . . . (1553).

⌐MARTIUS⌐
　He that would vouch it in any place but here.

TITUS
　What, would you bury him in my despite?

MARCUS
　No, noble Titus, but entreat of thee
　To pardon Mutius and to bury him.   370

TITUS
　Marcus, even thou hast struck upon my crest,
　And with these boys mine honor thou hast wounded.
　My foes I do repute you every one.
　So trouble me no more, but get you gone.

⌐QUINTUS⌐
　He is not with himself; let us withdraw.   375

⌐MARTIUS⌐
　Not I, till Mutius' bones be burièd.
　　　　　　　The brother (⌐Marcus⌐) and the sons
　　　　　　(⌐Lucius, Martius, and Quintus⌐) kneel.

MARCUS
　Brother, for in that name doth nature plead—

⌐MARTIUS⌐
　Father, and in that name doth nature speak—

TITUS
　Speak thou no more, if all the rest will speed.

MARCUS
　Renownèd Titus, more than half my soul—   380

LUCIUS
　Dear father, soul and substance of us all—

MARCUS
　Suffer thy brother Marcus to inter
　His noble nephew here in virtue's nest,
　That died in honor and Lavinia's cause.
　Thou art a Roman; be not barbarous.   385
　The Greeks upon advice did bury Ajax,
　That slew himself, and wise Laertes' son
　Did graciously plead for his funerals.

395. **friends':** relatives'
396. **trophies:** memorials
403. **device:** devising, scheming
404. **beholding:** beholden, obliged, indebted
405. **high:** extremely valuable; **good turn:** benefit
406. **remunerate:** reward, requite
407. **prize:** game
408. **gallant:** fine-looking

"Stately Phoebe 'mongst her nymphs." (1.1.322)
From Johann Engel, *Astrolabium* (1488).

Let not young Mutius, then, that was thy joy,
Be barred his entrance here.   390
TITUS   Rise, Marcus, rise.
                                                      ⌜*They rise.*⌝

The dismall'st day is this that e'er I saw,
To be dishonored by my sons in Rome.
Well, bury him, and bury me the next.
                        They put ⌜*Mutius*⌝ *in the tomb.*

LUCIUS
There lie thy bones, sweet Mutius, with thy friends',   395
Till we with trophies do adorn thy tomb.
                They all ⌜*except Titus*⌝ *kneel and say:*
No man shed tears for noble Mutius.
He lives in fame, that died in virtue's cause.
                        All but Marcus and Titus exit.

MARCUS
My lord, to step out of these dreary dumps,
How comes it that the subtle Queen of Goths   400
Is of a sudden thus advanced in Rome?
TITUS
I know not, Marcus, but I know it is.
Whether by device or no, the heavens can tell.
Is she not then beholding to the man
That brought her for this high good turn so far?   405
⟨Yes, and will nobly him remunerate.⟩

⟨*Flourish.*⟩ *Enter the Emperor* ⌜*Saturninus,*⌝ *Tamora
and her two sons, with* ⌜*Aaron*⌝ *the Moor,* ⌜*Drums and
    Trumpets,*⌝ *at one door. Enter at the other door
Bassianus and Lavinia, with* ⌜*Lucius, Martius, and
                Quintus, and*⌝ *others.*

SATURNINUS
So, Bassianus, you have played your prize.
God give you joy, sir, of your gallant bride.
BASSIANUS
And you of yours, my lord. I say no more,
Nor wish no less, and so I take my leave.   410

412. **rape:** abduction or violent seizure of a woman

416. **that:** i.e., that which

417, 418. **us, we:** i.e., me, I (the royal plural)

420. **Answer:** i.e., **answer** for it

421. **give . . . know:** i.e., tell **your Grace** so that you will **know**

424. **opinion:** reputation

427. **zeal:** devotion

428. **To be controlled:** i.e., in being restrained; **that:** i.e., that which; **frankly:** without restraint; generously

432. **leave:** cease

438. **indifferently:** impartially, without bias

439. **suit:** petition

A helmet with a crest. (1.1.371)
From Bonaventura Pistofilo, *Il torneo* . . . (1627).

SATURNINUS
  Traitor, if Rome have law or we have power,
  Thou and thy faction shall repent this rape.
BASSIANUS
  "Rape" call you it, my lord, to seize my own,
  My true betrothèd love and now my wife?
  But let the laws of Rome determine all.   415
  Meanwhile am I possessed of that is mine.
SATURNINUS
  'Tis good, sir, you are very short with us.
  But if we live, we'll be as sharp with you.
BASSIANUS
  My lord, what I have done, as best I may,
  Answer I must, and shall do with my life.   420
  Only thus much I give your Grace to know:
  By all the duties that I owe to Rome,
  This noble gentleman, Lord Titus here,
  Is in opinion and in honor wronged,
  That in the rescue of Lavinia   425
  With his own hand did slay his youngest son,
  In zeal to you, and highly moved to wrath
  To be controlled in that he frankly gave.
  Receive him then to favor, Saturnine,
  That hath expressed himself in all his deeds   430
  A father and a friend to thee and Rome.
TITUS
  Prince Bassianus, leave to plead my deeds.
  'Tis thou, and those, that have dishonored me.
  Rome and the righteous heavens be my judge
  How I have loved and honored Saturnine. ⌜*He kneels.*⌝ 435
TAMORA, ⌜*to Saturninus*⌝
  My worthy lord, if ever Tamora
  Were gracious in those princely eyes of thine,
  Then hear me speak indifferently for all,
  And at my suit, sweet, pardon what is past.

441. **put it up:** endure it patiently, submit to it

442. **forfend:** forbid

443. **author:** authorizer, instigator

444. **undertake:** make myself answerable or responsible; vouch

446. **not dissembled:** unconcealed; **griefs:** keen or bitter feelings; feelings of offense, displeasure

448. **suppose:** supposition

451. **won:** persuaded

452. **Dissemble:** conceal; **griefs:** grievances, injuries, feelings of offense

458. **entreats:** entreaties, supplications; **let me alone:** i.e., leave me to it

460. **raze:** obliterate (with possible wordplay on the archaic word *arace*, meaning "root out")

462. **sued:** pleaded

467. **Take up:** raise from his knees

A balance scale. (1.1.55)
From Silvestro Pietrasanta, . . . *Symbola heroica* . . . (1682).

SATURNINUS

  What, madam, be dishonored openly,   440

  And basely put it up without revenge?

TAMORA

  Not so, my lord; the gods of Rome forfend

  I should be author to dishonor you.

  But on mine honor dare I undertake

  For good Lord Titus' innocence in all,   445

  Whose fury not dissembled speaks his griefs.

  Then at my suit look graciously on him.

  Lose not so noble a friend on vain suppose,

  Nor with sour looks afflict his gentle heart.

  ⌜*Aside to Saturninus.*⌝ My lord, be ruled by me; be   450

    won at last.

  Dissemble all your griefs and discontents.

  You are but newly planted in your throne.

  Lest, then, the people, and patricians too,

  Upon a just survey take Titus' part   455

  And so supplant you for ingratitude,

  Which Rome reputes to be a heinous sin.

  Yield at entreats, and then let me alone.

  I'll find a day to massacre them all

  And raze their faction and their family,   460

  The cruel father and his traitorous sons,

  To whom I sued for my dear son's life,

  And make them know what 'tis to let a queen

  Kneel in the streets and beg for grace in vain.

  ⌜*Aloud.*⌝ Come, come, sweet emperor.—Come,   465

    Andronicus.—

  Take up this good old man, and cheer the heart

  That dies in tempest of thy angry frown.

SATURNINUS

  Rise, Titus, rise. My empress hath prevailed.

TITUS, ⌜*rising*⌝

  I thank your Majesty and her, my lord.   470

  These words, these looks, infuse new life in me.

472. **incorporate in:** united in one body with

473. **A Roman now adopted:** i.e., newly admitted to Roman status; **happily:** fortunately

485. **mildly as we might:** i.e., done as **mildly as we** could

486. **Tend'ring:** having concern for, valuing

487. **protest:** solemnly affirm or declare

493. **entreats:** entreaties, supplications

494. **remit:** forgive, pardon

TAMORA
  Titus, I am incorporate in Rome,
  A Roman now adopted happily,
  And must advise the Emperor for his good.
  This day all quarrels die, Andronicus.—   475
  And let it be mine honor, good my lord,
  That I have reconciled your friends and you.—
  For you, Prince Bassianus, I have passed
  My word and promise to the Emperor
  That you will be more mild and tractable.—   480
  And fear not, lords—and you, Lavinia.
  By my advice, all humbled on your knees,
  You shall ask pardon of his Majesty.
⌐*Marcus, Lavinia, Lucius, Martius, and Quintus kneel.*⌐
⌐LUCIUS⌐
  We do, and vow to heaven and to his Highness
  That what we did was mildly as we might,   485
  Tend'ring our sister's honor and our own.
MARCUS
  That on mine honor here do I protest.
SATURNINUS
  Away, and talk not; trouble us no more.
TAMORA
  Nay, nay, sweet emperor, we must all be friends.
  The tribune and his nephews kneel for grace.   490
  I will not be denied. Sweetheart, look back.
SATURNINUS
  Marcus, for thy sake, and thy brother's here,
  And at my lovely Tamora's entreats,
  I do remit these young men's heinous faults.
  Stand up.   ⌐*They rise.*⌐ 495
  Lavinia, though you left me like a churl,
  I found a friend, and sure as death I swore
  I would not part a bachelor from the priest.
  Come, if the Emperor's court can feast two brides,

500. **friends:** relatives

501. **love-day:** a **day** set aside for the amicable settlement of disputes (with wordplay on "a **day** for lovemaking")

502. **an it please:** if **it please**

504. **bonjour:** good day (French)

505. **gramercy:** thanks (from the Old French *grant merci*)

505 SD. **Sound . . . exit.:** See longer note, page 210.

Hunting the hart. (1.1.503)
From [George Turberville,] *The noble art of venerie or hunting . . .* (1611).

You are my guest, Lavinia, and your friends.— 500
This day shall be a love-day, Tamora.

TITUS

Tomorrow, an it please your Majesty
To hunt the panther and the hart with me,
With horn and hound we'll give your Grace *bonjour.*

SATURNINUS

Be it so, Titus, and gramercy too. 505

     Sound trumpets. All but Aaron exit.

TITUS ANDRONICUS

ACT 2

2.1 Aaron reveals that he is Tamora's lover, and then stops a fight between her sons, Chiron and Demetrius, who both want Lavinia. He encourages them to join in raping her.

————————

1. **Olympus' top:** i.e., the summit of Mount Olympus, home of the Greek gods
2. **Safe:** secure; **out:** beyond the range
3. **Secure of:** i.e., **secure** from (Homer's *Odyssey* describes the summit of Olympus as never disturbed by storms or drenched by rains [6.43–45].)
6. **gilt:** gilded, made golden
7. **Gallops:** i.e., **gallops** through; **glistering:** glittering (See picture, page 180.)
8. **overlooks:** rises above; **highest-peering hills:** i.e., **hills** that look up the **highest**
10. **wit:** intelligence; **wait:** attend
14. **mount her pitch:** fly up to the full height she has reached (**Pitch** is the highest point in a falcon's flight before it descends on its prey.) The phrase **mount her** carries inevitable sexual overtones.
16. **charming:** magically spellbinding
17. **Prometheus . . . Caucasus:** Zeus, king of the Greek gods, chained the Titan **Prometheus** to a rock in the **Caucasus** for daring to give the gift of fire to humankind. Each day a vulture gnawed away his liver, which grew again each night. (See picture, page 82.)
18. **weeds:** garments, clothes
21. **wanton:** play lewdly

(continued)

⟨ACT 2⟩

AARON
Now climbeth Tamora Olympus' top,
Safe out of Fortune's shot, and sits aloft,
Secure of thunder's crack or lightning flash,
Advanced above pale Envy's threat'ning reach.
As when the golden sun salutes the morn   5
And, having gilt the ocean with his beams,
Gallops the zodiac in his glistering coach
And overlooks the highest-peering hills,
So Tamora.
Upon her wit doth earthly honor wait,   10
And virtue stoops and trembles at her frown.
Then, Aaron, arm thy heart and fit thy thoughts
To mount aloft with thy imperial mistress,
And mount her pitch whom thou in triumph long
Hast prisoner held, fettered in amorous chains 15
And faster bound to Aaron's charming eyes
Than is Prometheus tied to Caucasus.
Away with slavish weeds and servile thoughts!
I will be bright, and shine in pearl and gold
To wait upon this new-made emperess.   20
To wait, said I? To wanton with this queen,
This goddess, this Semiramis, this nymph,
This siren that will charm Rome's Saturnine

49

22. **Semiramis:** legendary Assyrian queen, famous for her power, beauty, and lust (See picture, page 68.)

23. **siren:** one of a group of beautiful mythological women whose songs lured sailors to shipwreck (**shipwrack,** line 24); **charm:** cast a spell over

25 SD. **braving:** boasting, swaggering

26. **wants:** i.e., want, lack; **wit:** intelligence; **edge:** sharpness

27. **graced:** favorably received

28. **aught:** anything; **affected:** loved

29. **dost overween:** i.e., are arrogant, presumptuous

30. **bear me down:** overthrow me; **braves:** boasts

32. **gracious:** attractive, popular, acceptable

35. **approve:** prove

36. **passions:** desires

37. **Clubs, clubs:** an Elizabethan street cry to signal a brawl

38. **unadvised:** without reflection or consideration

39. **dancing rapier:** a light **sword** worn when dancing

40. **threat:** threaten

41. **Go to:** a dismissive expression; **lath:** wooden stage-sword

49. **wot:** know

And see his shipwrack and his commonweal's.
Holla! What storm is this? 25

Enter Chiron and Demetrius, braving.

DEMETRIUS
Chiron, thy years wants wit, thy wits wants edge
And manners, to intrude where I am graced,
And may, for aught thou knowest, affected be.
CHIRON
Demetrius, thou dost overween in all,
And so in this, to bear me down with braves. 30
'Tis not the difference of a year or two
Makes me less gracious or thee more fortunate.
I am as able and as fit as thou
To serve and to deserve my mistress' grace,
And that my sword upon thee shall approve 35
And plead my passions for Lavinia's love.
AARON, ⌐*aside*¬
Clubs, clubs! These lovers will not keep the peace.
DEMETRIUS, ⌐*to Chiron*¬
Why, boy, although our mother, unadvised,
Gave you a dancing rapier by your side,
Are you so desperate grown to threat your friends? 40
Go to. Have your lath glued within your sheath
Till you know better how to handle it.
CHIRON
Meanwhile, sir, with the little skill I have,
Full well shalt thou perceive how much I dare.
DEMETRIUS
Ay, boy, grow you so brave? *They draw.* 45
AARON Why, how now, lords?
So near the Emperor's palace dare you draw
And maintain such a quarrel openly?
Full well I wot the ground of all this grudge.
I would not for a million of gold 50
The cause were known to them it most concerns,

54. **put up:** i.e., sheathe your swords
56. **withal:** also
58. **breathed:** spoken
64. **brabble:** quarrel; **undo:** ruin, overthrow
66. **jet:** encroach
67. **What:** an interjection introducing a question
70. **controlment:** restraint, check
72. **ground:** reason, basis (with wordplay, signaled by **the music,** on the meaning of **ground** as "the bass over which a melody is played")
75. **Youngling:** youngster; **meaner:** lower, humbler
79. **competitors:** rivals
81. **device:** purpose, intention
83. **propose:** be ready to meet; confront

A cuckold. (2.1.93; 2.3.67; 4.3.74–77)
From *Bagford Ballads* (printed in 1878).

Nor would your noble mother for much more
Be so dishonored in the court of Rome.
For shame, put up.

DEMETRIUS   Not I, till I have sheathed   55
My rapier in his bosom, and withal
Thrust those reproachful speeches down his throat
That he hath breathed in my dishonor here.

CHIRON
For that I am prepared and full resolved,
Foul-spoken coward, that thund'rest with thy tongue   60
And with thy weapon nothing dar'st perform.

AARON   Away, I say!
Now by the gods that warlike Goths adore,
This petty brabble will undo us all.
Why, lords, and think you not how dangerous   65
It is to jet upon a prince's right?
What, is Lavinia then become so loose
Or Bassianus so degenerate
That for her love such quarrels may be broached
Without controlment, justice, or revenge?   70
Young lords, beware! And should the Empress know
This discord's ground, the music would not please.

CHIRON
I care not, I, knew she and all the world.
I love Lavinia more than all the world.

DEMETRIUS
Youngling, learn thou to make some meaner choice.   75
Lavinia is thine elder brother's hope.

AARON
Why, are you mad? Or know you not in Rome
How furious and impatient they be,
And cannot brook competitors in love?
I tell you, lords, you do but plot your deaths   80
By this device.

CHIRON   Aaron, a thousand deaths
Would I propose to achieve her whom I love.

85. **makes . . . strange:** do you pretend not to understand

86–87. **She is . . . won:** Proverbial: "All women **may be won.**"

89–90. **more . . . miller of:** proverbial (and suggesting that a married woman may have more sex than her husband knows of) **wots:** knows

91. **Of a cut . . . shive:** proverbial (suggesting that once a woman is not a virgin, no one can know the extent of her sexual activity) **shive:** slice

93. **Vulcan's badge:** cuckold's horns (See longer note, page 211, and picture, page 52.)

95. **to court it:** perhaps, how to act as courtier; or, perhaps, how to carry on a courtship

96. **liberality:** bountifulness, generosity

97. **struck:** killed with spear or arrow

98. **cleanly:** adroitly; **keeper's:** gamekeeper's

99. **snatch:** sudden grab; snack (used figuratively for sex)

100. **serve your turns:** (1) suit your purposes; (2) provide for your sexual needs

101. **turn:** Compare Shakespeare's *Antony and Cleopatra:* "the best **turn** i' th' bed" (2.5.72).

102. **hit it:** made the correct conjecture (with bawdy wordplay when **hit it** is repeated in line 103)

106. **square:** fall out, quarrel

107. **speed:** succeed

109. **so:** as long as

110. **join for that you jar:** i.e., come together to obtain **that for** which **you** quarrel

111. **policy:** cunning

112. **That you affect:** i.e., **that** which **you** desire

AARON
  To achieve her how?
DEMETRIUS   Why makes thou it so strange?   85
  She is a woman, therefore may be wooed;
  She is a woman, therefore may be won;
  She is Lavinia, therefore must be loved.
  What, man, more water glideth by the mill
  Than wots the miller of, and easy it is   90
  Of a cut loaf to steal a shive, we know.
  Though Bassianus be the Emperor's brother,
  Better than he have worn Vulcan's badge.
AARON, ⌈*aside*⌉
  Ay, and as good as Saturninus may.
DEMETRIUS
  Then why should he despair that knows to court it   95
  With words, fair looks, and liberality?
  What, hast not thou full often struck a doe
  And borne her cleanly by the keeper's nose?
AARON
  Why, then, it seems some certain snatch or so
  Would serve your turns.   100
CHIRON   Ay, so the turn were served.
DEMETRIUS   Aaron, thou hast hit it.
AARON   Would you had hit it too!
  Then should not we be tired with this ado.
  Why, hark you, hark you! And are you such fools   105
  To square for this? Would it offend you then
  That both should speed?
CHIRON
  Faith, not me.
DEMETRIUS   Nor me, so I were one.
AARON
  For shame, be friends, and join for that you jar.   110
  'Tis policy and stratagem must do
  That you affect, and so must you resolve

113–14. **what . . . may:** Proverbial: "Men must do as they **may** (can), not as they would."

115. **Lucrece:** a Roman matron who exemplified married chastity (When raped, **Lucrece** committed suicide.) See picture, page 72.

119. **solemn:** ceremonious; **in hand:** in process

120. **troop:** gather; walk

122. **plots:** patches

123. **kind:** nature

124. **Single:** separate from the herd

125. **strike her home:** i.e., conquer her (literally, kill or wound her with spear or arrow) **home:** effectively, thoroughly

127. **sacred:** accursed (a rare meaning that draws on an ironic use of the word *sacra*, meaning "sacred," in Virgil's Latin *auri sacra fames*—"sacred hunger for gold" [*Aeneid* 3.57])

128. **consecrate:** devoted

129. **withal:** with

130. **file:** elaborate to perfection; **engines:** plots, snares

131. **square yourselves:** quarrel

133. **Fame:** i.e., rumor (Chaucer's poem *Hous of Fame* was well-known in Shakespeare's time.)

135. **dull:** cheerless

141. **Sit fas aut nefas:** be it right or wrong (Latin)

142. **charm:** action with magical powers

143. **Per Stygia, per manes vehor:** I am borne through Stygian regions [the underworld of classical mythology, Hades] among shades [disembodied spirits] (Latin).

That what you cannot as you would achieve,
You must perforce accomplish as you may.
Take this of me: Lucrece was not more chaste   115
Than this Lavinia, Bassianus' love.
A speedier course ⌜than⌝ ling'ring languishment
Must we pursue, and I have found the path.
My lords, a solemn hunting is in hand;
There will the lovely Roman ladies troop.   120
The forest walks are wide and spacious,
And many unfrequented plots there are,   *encouraging*
Fitted by kind for rape and villainy.   *Chiron & Demetrius*
Single you thither then this dainty doe,   *to rape her*
And strike her home by force, if not by words.   125
This way, or not at all, stand you in hope.
Come, come, our empress, with her sacred wit
To villainy and vengeance consecrate,
Will we acquaint withal what we intend,
And she shall file our engines with advice   130
That will not suffer you to square yourselves,
But to your wishes' height advance you both.
The Emperor's court is like the house of Fame,
The palace full of tongues, of eyes, and ears;
The woods are ruthless, dreadful, deaf, and dull.   135
There speak and strike, brave boys, and take your
    turns.
There serve your lust, shadowed from heaven's eye,
And revel in Lavinia's treasury.

CHIRON
Thy counsel, lad, smells of no cowardice.   140

DEMETRIUS
Sit fas aut nefas, till I find the stream
To cool this heat, a charm to calm these fits,
Per Stygia, per manes vehor.
                                        They exit.

2.2 As the morning hunt gets under way, Demetrius and Chiron anticipate raping Lavinia.

---

0 SD. **noise:** melodious sound

1. **The hunt is up:** a phrase that recalls the popular early morning song "Hunt's Up"; **gray:** a word often used to describe the sky at twilight or in the early morning

3. **Uncouple:** i.e., set free the hounds for the hunt (For possible stagings of this scene, see longer note, page 211.) **make a bay:** i.e., have the hounds bark deep and long

5. **peal:** loud outburst of sound (here made by blowing hunters' horns)

8. **attend:** wait on; **carefully:** attentively

9. **this night:** i.e., this past night

10 SD. **cry:** yelping; **wind:** blow

11. **morrows:** mornings

14. **rung:** sounded

⌈Scene 2⌉

Enter Titus Andronicus and his three sons, ⌈and
Marcus,⌉ making a noise with hounds and horns.

TITUS
  The hunt is up, the moon is bright and gray,
  The fields are fragrant, and the woods are green.
  Uncouple here, and let us make a bay
  And wake the Emperor and his lovely bride,
  And rouse the Prince, and ring a hunter's peal,   5
  That all the court may echo with the noise.
  Sons, let it be your charge, as it is ours,
  To attend the Emperor's person carefully.
  I have been troubled in my sleep this night,
  But dawning day new comfort hath inspired.   10

Here a cry of hounds, and wind horns in a peal. Then
enter Saturninus, Tamora, Bassianus, Lavinia, Chiron,
Demetrius, and their Attendants.

TITUS
  Many good morrows to your Majesty;—
  Madam, to you as many, and as good.—
  I promisèd your Grace a hunter's peal.
SATURNINUS
  And you have rung it lustily, my lords—
  Somewhat too early for new-married ladies.   15
BASSIANUS
  Lavinia, how say you?
LAVINIA   I say no.
  I have been broad awake two hours and more.
SATURNINUS
  Come on, then. Horse and chariots let us have,
  And to our sport. (⌈*To Tamora*⌉) Madam, now shall   20
    you see
  Our Roman hunting.
MARCUS   I have dogs, my lord,

24. **Will rouse:** that will startle from cover; **proudest:** most magnificent; most spirited; **chase:** hunting ground

25. **promontory:** mountain ridge (the literal meaning of the Latin *promunturium*)

26. **horse:** i.e., horses

2.3 Aaron sets a trap to destroy Bassianus and put the blame on Titus's sons Quintus and Martius. He has Tamora quarrel with Lavinia and Bassianus, a quarrel that ends in Bassianus's death at the hands of Chiron and Demetrius, who carry off Lavinia. Aaron then brings Quintus and Martius to the pit where Bassianus's body lies and, using a forged letter and hidden gold, makes them appear guilty of the murder.

––––––––––

1. **wit:** intelligence

2. **under a tree:** i.e., **among the nettles at the elder tree** (line 273 below)

3. **inherit:** take possession of

4. **thinks . . . abjectly:** i.e., has such a base opinion of me

5. **coin:** devise (with obvious wordplay)

8. **unrest:** trouble

9. **have . . . chest:** i.e., receive the **alms** (of this gold) from Tamora's treasury

10. **wherefore:** why

11. **doth . . . boast:** i.e., delights in its glory

13. **rollèd:** coiled

17. **babbling: Hounds** whose cry is uncontrolled are said to "babble." Here, the **babbling** is transferred to the **echo** of **the hounds.**

Will rouse the proudest panther in the chase
And climb the highest promontory top.   25

TITUS
  And I have horse will follow where the game
  Makes way and runs like swallows o'er the plain.

DEMETRIUS, ⌈*aside to Chiron*⌉
  Chiron, we hunt not, we, with horse nor hound,
  But hope to pluck a dainty doe to ground.

                                        They exit.

              ⌈Scene 3⌉

    Enter Aaron, alone, ⌈carrying a bag of gold.⌉

AARON
  He that had wit would think that I had none,
  To bury so much gold under a tree
  And never after to inherit it.
  Let him that thinks of me so abjectly
  Know that this gold must coin a stratagem   5
  Which, cunningly effected, will beget
  A very excellent piece of villainy.   ⌈*He hides the bag.*⌉
  And so repose, sweet gold, for their unrest
  That have their alms out of the Empress' chest.

    Enter Tamora alone to ⌈Aaron⌉ the Moor.

TAMORA
  My lovely Aaron, wherefore look'st thou sad,   10
  When everything doth make a gleeful boast?
  The birds chant melody on every bush,
  The snakes lies rollèd in the cheerful sun,
  The green leaves quiver with the cooling wind
  And make a checkered shadow on the ground.   15
  Under their sweet shade, Aaron, let us sit,
  And whilst the babbling echo mocks the hounds,

20. **mark:** pay attention to; **yellowing:** yelping, bellowing, baying

22. **wand'ring prince and Dido:** Aeneas, **prince** of fallen Troy, **wand'ring** the Mediterranean, came to the shores of Carthage, where he met its queen, **Dido.** While they were hunting, a storm overtook them, and they sought refuge in a cave, where they first made love (Virgil, *Aeneid* 4.160–72). See longer note, page 211, and picture, page 102.

23. **happy:** fortunate

24. **counsel-keeping:** secret-keeping

28. **nurse's:** i.e., wet **nurse's**

30. **Venus:** Roman goddess of love

31. **Saturn . . . mine:** i.e., **Saturn is** the prime astrological influence **over** my **desires** (Men under Saturn's influence were thought by Elizabethans to be gloomy—see **sad** in line 10 and **cloudy melancholy** in line 33—and vengeful.) See picture, page 74.

32. **deadly standing:** murderously fixed

35. **unroll:** uncoil

36. **execution:** action

37. **venereal:** associated with Venus and with sexual desire

41. **hopes:** i.e., **hopes** for

43. **Philomel:** an Athenian princess raped by her brother-in-law King Tereus of Thrace, who cut out her tongue to prevent her from disclosing his crime (See Appendix.)

47. **fatal-plotted:** i.e., devised to be deadly

48. **espied:** observed, seen

49. **parcel:** group; **hopeful:** hoped-for

50. **dreads not yet:** does **not yet** fearfully anticipate

Replying shrilly to the well-tuned horns,
As if a double hunt were heard at once,
Let us sit down and mark their yellowing noise.   20
And after conflict such as was supposed
The wand'ring prince and Dido once enjoyed
When with a happy storm they were surprised,
And curtained with a counsel-keeping cave,
We may, each wreathèd in the other's arms,   25
Our pastimes done, possess a golden slumber,
Whiles hounds and horns and sweet melodious birds
Be unto us as is a nurse's song
Of lullaby to bring her babe asleep.

AARON
Madam, though Venus govern your desires,   30
Saturn is dominator over mine.
What signifies my deadly standing eye,
My silence, and my cloudy melancholy,
My fleece of woolly hair that now uncurls
Even as an adder when she doth unroll   35
To do some fatal execution?
No, madam, these are no venereal signs.
Vengeance is in my heart, death in my hand,
Blood and revenge are hammering in my head.
Hark, Tamora, the empress of my soul,   40
Which never hopes more heaven than rests in thee,
This is the day of doom for Bassianus.
His Philomel must lose her tongue today,
Thy sons make pillage of her chastity
And wash their hands in Bassianus' blood.   45
                         ⌜*He takes out a paper.*⌝
Seest thou this letter? Take it up, I pray thee,
And give the King this fatal-plotted scroll.
                         ⌜*He hands her the paper.*⌝
Now, question me no more. We are espied.
Here comes a parcel of our hopeful booty,
Which dreads not yet their lives' destruction.   50

53. **cross:** quarrelsome

56. **Unfurnished . . . troop:** without her appropriate company

57. **Dian:** i.e., Diana, Roman goddess of chastity and the hunt (See picture, page 70.) **habited:** dressed

59. **general hunting:** i.e., hunt in which all take part

60. **Saucy:** insolent; **controller:** censorious critic

62–64. **Thy temples . . . limbs:** i.e., you would be turned into a hart, as Acteon was by Diana after he saw her bathing. Your head, too, would immediately bear **horns,** and you, too, would be torn apart by **hounds.** (See picture, page 80.) **presently:** immediately **drive:** rush

66. **Under your patience:** a polite phrase requesting permission

67. **horning:** cuckolding (See longer note to 2.1.93, page 211.)

68. **doubted:** suspected

69. **Are singled forth:** have drawn aside

71. **'Tis pity they should take:** i.e., it would be a **pity** if they took

72. **Cimmerian:** a term that meant both a nomadic outsider (one of the Cimmerii, an ancient nomadic tribe) and one who dwells in utter darkness (a member of a legendary tribe in Homer's *Odyssey*)

74. **Spotted:** morally stained or blemished; **abominable:** loathsome (spelled "abhominable" in the 1594 Quarto, a spelling that indicates the false belief of the Elizabethans that the word derives from the Latin *ab homine,* or "apart from man," i.e., inhuman)

77. **plot:** spot

Enter Bassianus and Lavinia.

TAMORA
  Ah, my sweet Moor, sweeter to me than life!
AARON
  No more, great empress. Bassianus comes.
  Be cross with him, and I'll go fetch thy sons
  To back thy quarrels, whatsoe'er they be.
                                    ⌐*He exits.*⌐

BASSIANUS
  Who have we here? Rome's royal empress,   55
  Unfurnished of her well-beseeming troop?
  Or is it Dian, habited like her,
  Who hath abandonèd her holy groves
  To see the general hunting in this forest?
TAMORA
  Saucy controller of my private steps,   60
  Had I the power that some say Dian had,
  Thy temples should be planted presently
  With horns, as was Acteon's, and the hounds
  Should drive upon thy new-transformèd limbs,
  Unmannerly intruder as thou art.   65
LAVINIA
  Under your patience, gentle empress,
  'Tis thought you have a goodly gift in horning,
  And to be doubted that your Moor and you
  Are singled forth to try experiments.
  Jove shield your husband from his hounds today!   70
  'Tis pity they should take him for a stag.
BASSIANUS
  Believe me, queen, your swarthy Cimmerian
  Doth make your honor of his body's hue,
  Spotted, detested, and abominable.
  Why are you sequestered from all your train,   75
  Dismounted from your snow-white goodly steed,
  And wandered hither to an obscure plot,

80. **sport:** amorous play
81. **rated:** chided
82. **sauciness:** insolence
83. **joy:** enjoy
84. **passing:** surpassingly, exceedingly
86. **slips:** offenses, moral transgressions; **noted:** specially marked (i.e., notorious as a cuckold)
87. **abused:** deceived; wronged
92. **ticed:** enticed
93. **detested:** odious
94. **lean:** poor, meager, thin
95. **Overcome:** covered, overrun; **mistletoe:** called **baleful** (destructive) because it is parasitic
97. **fatal:** ominous
99. **at dead time of the night:** i.e., in the dead of the **night   dead:** profoundly quiet or still
101. **urchins:** hedgehogs; goblins, elves
102. **fearful:** terrible, dreadful
103. **As:** i.e., that
104. **straight:** straightaway, immediately

Accompanied but with a barbarous Moor,
If foul desire had not conducted you?

LAVINIA
And being intercepted in your sport,   80
Great reason that my noble lord be rated
For sauciness.—I pray you, let us hence,
And let her joy her raven-colored love.
This valley fits the purpose passing well.

BASSIANUS
The King my brother shall have notice of this.   85

LAVINIA
'Ay, for these slips have made him noted long.
Good king to be so mightily abused!

TAMORA
Why, I have patience to endure all this.

Enter Chiron and Demetrius.

DEMETRIUS
How now, dear sovereign and our gracious mother,
Why doth your Highness look so pale and wan?   90

TAMORA
Have I not reason, think you, to look pale?
These two have ticed me hither to this place,
A barren, detested vale you see it is;
The trees, though summer, yet forlorn and lean,
Overcome with moss and baleful mistletoe.   95
Here never shines the sun, here nothing breeds,
Unless the nightly owl or fatal raven.
And when they showed me this abhorrèd pit,
They told me, here at dead time of the night
A thousand fiends, a thousand hissing snakes,   100
Ten thousand swelling toads, as many urchins,
Would make such fearful and confusèd cries
As any mortal body hearing it
Should straight fall mad, or else die suddenly.
No sooner had they told this hellish tale   105

117. **struck home:** penetrating as deeply as possible

118. **Semiramis:** See note to 2.1.22 and picture below.

120. **poniard:** dagger (See picture, page 84.)

122. **belongs to:** concerns

123. **thrash:** thresh

124. **minion:** hussy; **stood upon:** made a point of; insisted on

126. **painted:** i.e., false

130. **trunk:** body, corpse

132. **outlive:** survive

Semiramis. (2.1.22; 2.3.118)
*From Le microcosme contenant diuers tableaux
de la vie humaine . . . [n.d.].*

But straight they told me they would bind me here
Unto the body of a dismal yew
And leave me to this miserable death.
And then they called me foul adulteress,
Lascivious Goth, and all the bitterest terms   110
That ever ear did hear to such effect.
And had you not by wondrous fortune come,
This vengeance on me had they executed.
Revenge it as you love your mother's life,
Or be you not henceforth called my children.   115

DEMETRIUS, ⌜*drawing his dagger*⌝
This is a witness that I am thy son.

CHIRON, ⌜*drawing his dagger*⌝
And this for me, struck home to show my strength.
                              ⌜*They*⌝ stab ⌜*Bassianus.*⌝

LAVINIA
Ay, come, Semiramis, nay, barbarous Tamora,
For no name fits thy nature but thy own!

TAMORA
Give me the poniard! You shall know, my boys,   120
Your mother's hand shall right your mother's wrong.

DEMETRIUS
Stay, madam, here is more belongs to her.
First thrash the corn, then after burn the straw.
This minion stood upon her chastity,
Upon her nuptial vow, her loyalty,   125
And with that painted hope braves your mightiness;
And shall she carry this unto her grave?

CHIRON
And if she do, I would I were an eunuch!
Drag hence her husband to some secret hole,
And make his dead trunk pillow to our lust.   130

TAMORA
But when you have the honey ⌜you⌝ desire,
Let not this wasp outlive, us both to sting.

CHIRON
I warrant you, madam, we will make that sure.—

135. **nice:** fastidiously, carefully, scrupulously; **honesty:** chastity

142. **dam:** mother

143. **learn:** teach

144. **suck'st:** i.e., sucked'st (did suck)

145. **thy teat:** i.e., the **teat** you sucked; **tyranny:** violence, outrage, villainy

150. **find it:** i.e., **find it** so

151–52. **The lion . . . away:** a story from Aesop's fables that had become proverbial   **paws:** i.e., claws (metonymy)

153. **forlorn:** abandoned; **children:** i.e., young birds

154. **birds:** i.e., young ones

156. **Nothing:** not at all; **something:** somewhat

157. **it:** perhaps, pity

Diana, with a stag at her feet. (2.3.57–59, 61)
From Robert Whitcombe, *Janua diuorum* . . . (1678).

Come, mistress, now perforce we will enjoy
That nice-preservèd honesty of yours.   135

LAVINIA
O Tamora, thou bearest a woman's face—

TAMORA
I will not hear her speak. Away with her.

LAVINIA
Sweet lords, entreat her hear me but a word.

DEMETRIUS, ⌜*to Tamora*⌝
Listen, fair madam. Let it be your glory
To see her tears, but be your heart to them   140
As unrelenting flint to drops of rain.

LAVINIA
When did the tiger's young ones teach the dam?
O, do not learn her wrath; she taught it thee.
The milk thou suck'st from her did turn to marble.
Even at thy teat thou hadst thy tyranny.   145
Yet every mother breeds not sons alike.
⌜*To Chiron.*⌝ Do thou entreat her show a woman's pity.

CHIRON
What, wouldst thou have me prove myself a bastard?

LAVINIA
'Tis true; the raven doth not hatch a lark.
Yet have I heard—O, could I find it now!—   150
The lion, moved with pity, did endure
To have his princely paws pared all away.
Some say that ravens foster forlorn children,
The whilst their own birds famish in their nests.
O, be to me, though thy hard heart say no,   155
Nothing so kind, but something pitiful.

TAMORA
I know not what it means.—Away with her.

LAVINIA
O, let me teach thee! For my father's sake,
That gave thee life when well he might have slain thee,
Be not obdurate; open thy deaf ⌜ears.⌝   160

162. **Even:** just, precisely

167. **of me:** i.e., by me

172. **Fond . . . go:** Lavinia may have knelt and clasped Tamora's knees, or have taken her hand or arm.   **Fond:** foolish

173. **present:** immediate

174. **denies:** forbids

181. **stayed:** delayed

183. **our general name:** i.e., the **name** of **womanhood**

184. **Confusion:** destruction, ruin

185. **stop your mouth:** gag or muzzle you

Chaste Lucrece. (2.1.115)
From Silvestro Pietrasanta, . . . *Symbola heroica* . . . (1682).

TAMORA
 Hadst thou in person ne'er offended me,
 Even for his sake am I pitiless.—
 Remember, boys, I poured forth tears in vain
 To save your brother from the sacrifice,
 But fierce Andronicus would not relent.   165
 Therefore away with her, and use her as you will;
 The worse to her, the better loved of me.

LAVINIA
 O Tamora, be called a gentle queen,
 And with thine own hands kill me in this place!
 For 'tis not life that I have begged so long;   170
 Poor I was slain when Bassianus died.

TAMORA
 What begg'st thou, then? Fond woman, let me go!

LAVINIA
 'Tis present death I beg, and one thing more
 That womanhood denies my tongue to tell.
 O, keep me from their worse-than-killing lust,   175
 And tumble me into some loathsome pit
 Where never man's eye may behold my body.
 Do this, and be a charitable murderer.

TAMORA
 So should I rob my sweet sons of their fee.
 No, let them satisfy their lust on thee.   180

DEMETRIUS, ⌜to Lavinia⌝
 Away, for thou hast stayed us here too long!

LAVINIA, ⌜to Tamora⌝
 No grace, no womanhood? Ah, beastly creature,
 The blot and enemy to our general name,
 Confusion fall—

CHIRON
 Nay, then, I'll stop your mouth.—Bring thou her   185
   husband.
 This is the hole where Aaron bid us hide him.
                    ⌜*They put Bassianus' body in the pit and*
                              exit, carrying off Lavinia.⌝

188. **make her sure:** kill her
189. **cheer:** mood
190. **made away:** killed
192. **spleenful:** passionate; **deflower:** ravish
193. **the better foot before:** i.e., make haste (Proverbial: "Set forth **the better foot.**")
195. **espied:** observed
199. **subtle:** cleverly designed
200. **rude-growing:** wild
202. **fresh:** bright and clear
203. **fatal:** ominous; deadly
205. **dismal'st:** most calamitous, most wretched; **object:** sight, spectacle

Saturn. (2.3.31; 4.3.58)
From Abu Ma'shar, *De magnis coniunctionibus* . . . [1515].

74

TAMORA

    Farewell, my sons. See that you make her sure.

    Ne'er let my heart know merry cheer indeed

    Till all the Andronici be made away.   190

    Now will I hence to seek my lovely Moor,

    And let my spleenful sons this trull deflower.

                              ⟨*She exits.*⟩

         Enter Aaron with two of Titus' sons,
             ⌜*Quintus and Martius.*⌝

⟨AARON⟩

    Come on, my lords, the better foot before.

    Straight will I bring you to the loathsome pit

    Where I espied the panther fast asleep.   195

QUINTUS

    My sight is very dull, whate'er it bodes.

MARTIUS

    And mine, I promise you. Were it not for shame,

    Well could I leave our sport to sleep awhile.

                      ⌜*He falls into the pit.*⌝

QUINTUS

    What, art thou fallen? What subtle hole is this,

    Whose mouth is covered with rude-growing briers   200

    Upon whose leaves are drops of new-shed blood

    As fresh as morning dew distilled on flowers?

    A very fatal place it seems to me.

    Speak, brother! Hast thou hurt thee with the fall?

MARTIUS

    O, brother, with the dismal'st object hurt   205

    That ever eye with sight made heart lament!

AARON, ⌜*aside*⌝

    Now will I fetch the King to find them here,

    That he thereby may have a likely guess

    How these were they that made away his brother.

                             He exits.

212. **surprisèd with:** overcome by; **uncouth:** unknown, strange

217. **fearful:** dreadful, horrible

220. **surmise:** i.e., imagining (it)

223. **berayed in:** defiled by

224. **on a heap:** prostrate

228. **ring that lightens:** According to Elizabethan belief, some jewels shone in the dark. **lightens:** illuminates

229. **monument:** tomb

230. **earthy:** i.e., earthlike

231. **ragged:** rough (having a broken, jagged surface); **entrails:** interior

232. **Pyramus:** legendary figure who killed himself thinking his beloved Thisbe was dead (Shakespeare's *A Midsummer Night's Dream*, Act 5, includes a comic dramatization of the story.) See picture, page 78.

233. **maiden blood:** perhaps, Thisbe's **blood** (in which case, this would be after Thisbe stabs herself on finding Pyramus's body); or, perhaps, Pyramus's **blood** (The words *maid* and *virgin* were used to refer to chaste young men as well as women. See, e.g., *Twelfth Night* 5.1.275.)

236. **fell:** terrible, dreadful

237. **Cocytus' misty mouth: Cocytus** is one of the rivers in the classical underworld of Hades. See longer note, page 212.

MARTIUS
  Why dost not comfort me and help me out   210
  From this ⌐unhallowed¬ and bloodstainèd hole?

QUINTUS
  I am surprisèd with an uncouth fear.
  A chilling sweat o'erruns my trembling joints.
  My heart suspects more than mine eye can see.

MARTIUS
  To prove thou hast a true-divining heart,   215
  Aaron and thou look down into this den
  And see a fearful sight of blood and death.

QUINTUS
  Aaron is gone, and my compassionate heart
  Will not permit mine eyes once to behold
  The thing whereat it trembles by surmise.   220
  O, tell me who it is, for ne'er till now
  Was I a child to fear I know not what.

MARTIUS
  Lord Bassianus lies ⌐berayed¬ in blood,
  All on a heap, like to a slaughtered lamb,
  In this detested, dark, blood-drinking pit.   225

QUINTUS
  If it be dark, how dost thou know 'tis he?

MARTIUS
  Upon his bloody finger he doth wear
  A precious ring that lightens all this hole,
  Which like a taper in some monument
  Doth shine upon the dead man's earthy cheeks   230
  And shows the ragged entrails of this pit.
  So pale did shine the moon on Pyramus
  When he by night lay bathed in maiden blood.
  O, brother, help me with thy fainting hand—
  If fear hath made thee faint as me it hath—   235
  Out of this fell devouring receptacle,
  As hateful as ⌐Cocytus'¬ misty mouth.

239. **wanting:** lacking
244. **loose:** i.e., let loose
247. **Along with me:** i.e., come along
256. **chase:** hunting ground
259. **out alas:** an exclamation of lamentation

Pyramus and Thisbe. (2.3.232–33)
From Gabriele Simeoni, *La vita* . . . (1559).

QUINTUS, ⌈*reaching into the pit*⌉
    Reach me thy hand, that I may help thee out,
    Or, wanting strength to do thee so much good,
    I may be plucked into the swallowing womb   240
    Of this deep pit, poor Bassianus' grave.
                      ⌈*He pulls Martius' hand.*⌉
    I have no strength to pluck thee to the brink.

MARTIUS
    Nor I no strength to climb without thy help.

QUINTUS
    Thy hand once more. I will not loose again
    Till thou art here aloft or I below.   245
    Thou canst not come to me. I come to thee.
                        ⌈*He falls in.*⌉

    Enter the Emperor ⌈*Saturninus, with Attendants,*⌉
               and Aaron the Moor.

SATURNINUS
    Along with me! I'll see what hole is here
    And what he is that now is leapt into it.—
    Say, who art thou that lately didst descend
    Into this gaping hollow of the earth?   250

MARTIUS
    The unhappy sons of old Andronicus,
    Brought hither in a most unlucky hour
    To find thy brother Bassianus dead.

SATURNINUS
    My brother dead! I know thou dost but jest.
    He and his lady both are at the lodge   255
    Upon the north side of this pleasant chase.
    'Tis not an hour since I left them there.

MARTIUS
    We know not where you left them all alive,
    But, out alas, here have we found him dead.

    Enter Tamora, ⌈*Titus*⌉ *Andronicus, and Lucius.*

263. **search:** probe
265. **fatal:** deadly, ominous; **writ:** writing, letter
266. **complot:** plot; **timeless:** untimely; eternal
267. **fold:** i.e., conceal (by analogy with *unfold*, meaning "reveal")
268. **tyranny:** villainy
269. **An if:** if; **handsomely:** conveniently
282. **fell:** savage; **kind:** nature

The transformed Acteon attacked by his hounds. (2.3.63)
From Henry Peacham, *Minerua Britanna* . . . (1612).

TAMORA   Where is my lord the King?   260
SATURNINUS
  Here, Tamora, though grieved with killing grief.
TAMORA
  Where is thy brother Bassianus?
SATURNINUS
  Now to the bottom dost thou search my wound.
  Poor Bassianus here lies murderèd.
TAMORA
  Then all too late I bring this fatal writ,   265
  The complot of this timeless tragedy,
  And wonder greatly that man's face can fold
  In pleasing smiles such murderous tyranny.
                          She giveth Saturnine a letter.
SATURNINUS (*reads the letter*):
  An if we miss to meet him handsomely,
  Sweet huntsman—Bassianus 'tis we mean—   270
  Do thou so much as dig the grave for him;
  Thou know'st our meaning. Look for thy reward
  Among the nettles at the elder tree
  Which overshades the mouth of that same pit
  Where we decreed to bury Bassianus.   275
  Do this, and purchase us thy lasting friends.
  O Tamora, was ever heard the like?
  This is the pit, and this the elder tree.—
  Look, sirs, if you can find the huntsman out
  That should have murdered Bassianus here.   280
AARON
  My gracious lord, here is the bag of gold.
SATURNINUS, ⌜*to Titus*⌝
  Two of thy whelps, fell curs of bloody kind,
  Have here bereft my brother of his life.—
  Sirs, drag them from the pit unto the prison.
  There let them bide until we have devised   285
  Some never-heard-of torturing pain for them.

291. **fault:** offense
293. **apparent:** obvious
299. **their suspicion:** i.e., the **suspicion** they are under
306. **Fear not:** i.e., **fear not** for

The chained Prometheus gnawed
by a vulture. (2.1.17; 5.2.32)
From Geoffrey Whitney, *A choice of emblemes* . . . (1586).

TAMORA
    What, are they in this pit? O wondrous thing!
    How easily murder is discoverèd.
            ⌜*Attendants pull Quintus, Martius, and*
               the body of Bassianus from the pit.⌝

TITUS, ⌜*kneeling*⌝
    High Emperor, upon my feeble knee
    I beg this boon with tears not lightly shed,   290
    That this fell fault of my accursèd sons—
    Accursèd if the faults be proved in them—

SATURNINUS
    If it be proved! You see it is apparent.
    Who found this letter? Tamora, was it you?

TAMORA
    Andronicus himself did take it up.   295

TITUS
    I did, my lord, yet let me be their bail,
    For by my father's reverend tomb I vow
    They shall be ready at your Highness' will
    To answer their suspicion with their lives.

SATURNINUS
    Thou shalt not bail them. See thou follow me.—   300
    Some bring the murdered body, some the murderers.
    Let them not speak a word. The guilt is plain.
    For, by my soul, were there worse end than death,
    That end upon them should be executed.

TAMORA
    Andronicus, I will entreat the King.   305
    Fear not thy sons; they shall do well enough.

TITUS, ⌜*rising*⌝
    Come, Lucius, come. Stay not to talk with them.
        ⟨*They exit,*⟩ ⌜*with Attendants leading Martius and*
           Quintus and bearing the body of Bassianus.⌝

2.4   The raped and mutilated Lavinia is discovered by her horrified uncle, Marcus.

———————

1. **an if:** i.e., **if**
3. **bewray:** divulge, disclose
5. **scrowl:** perhaps a version of *scrawl,* which could mean "gesticulate" (*Scrawl* could also, of course, mean "write awkwardly," although this meaning is not otherwise recorded until the seventeenth century.)
6. **sweet:** fragrant, perfumed; or, perhaps, simply fresh
9. **An 'twere:** if it were; **cause:** case
10. **knit:** tie a knot in
12. **Cousin:** term of address for almost any close relative
13. **would all . . . wake me:** i.e., I would forfeit all I have to be able to awake
14. **strike me down:** i.e., exert its malignant influence on me
16. **stern:** merciless, cruel

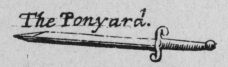

The Ponyard.

A poniard. (2.3.120)
From Louis de Gaya, *A treatise of the arms . . .* (1678).

84

⌜Scene 4⌝

Enter the Empress' sons, ⌜Demetrius and Chiron,⌝
with Lavinia, her hands cut off, and her tongue cut out,
and ravished.

DEMETRIUS
So, now go tell, an if thy tongue can speak,
Who 'twas that cut thy tongue and ravished thee.
CHIRON
Write down thy mind; bewray thy meaning so,
An if thy stumps will let thee play the scribe.
DEMETRIUS
See how with signs and tokens she can scrowl.   5
CHIRON, ⌜to Lavinia⌝
Go home. Call for sweet water; wash thy hands.
DEMETRIUS
She hath no tongue to call, nor hands to wash;
And so let's leave her to her silent walks.
CHIRON
An 'twere my cause, I should go hang myself.
DEMETRIUS
If thou hadst hands to help thee knit the cord.   10
⌜*Chiron and Demetrius*⌝ *exit.*

Enter Marcus from hunting.

⌜MARCUS⌝
Who is this? My niece, that flies away so fast?—
Cousin, a word. Where is your husband?
If I do dream, would all my wealth would wake me.
If I do wake, some planet strike me down
That I may slumber an eternal sleep.   15
Speak, gentle niece. What stern ungentle hands
Hath lopped and hewed and made thy body bare
Of her two branches, those sweet ornaments
Whose circling shadows kings have sought to sleep in,
And might not gain so great a happiness   20
As half thy love? Why dost not speak to me?

24. **rosèd lips:** rose-colored **lips** (or, perhaps, **lips** made red by the **blood**)

26. **Tereus:** See note to 2.3.43 and Appendix.

27. **detect:** expose; accuse

31. **Titan's:** the sun's (See note to 1.1.228.)

34. **heart:** the seat of thought, as well as feeling

36–37. **Sorrow ... it is:** Proverbial: "An oven dammed up bakes soonest." **stopped:** shut up

38–39. **Fair Philomela ... sewed her mind:** Tongueless and imprisoned by her rapist King Tereus, Philomela embroidered a tapestry that revealed his identity as her assailant. (See Appendix.) **tedious:** i.e., laboriously executed **sampler:** piece of embroidery

40. **that mean is:** i.e., those means are

51. **Cerberus:** the three-headed dog that guards the gates to Hades (It **fell asleep** charmed by the music of the **Thracian** poet Orpheus when he came to Hades to recover his bride, Eurydice.) See pictures below and on page 100.

54. **meads:** meadows

55. **tears thy:** i.e., **tears** do to **thy**

Cerberus. (2.4.51)
From Vincenzo Cartari, *Imagines deorum* ... (1581).

Alas, a crimson river of warm blood,
Like to a bubbling fountain stirred with wind,
Doth rise and fall between thy rosèd lips,
Coming and going with thy honey breath.   25
But sure some Tereus hath deflowered thee,
And lest thou shouldst detect ⌜him⌝ cut thy tongue.
Ah, now thou turn'st away thy face for shame,
And notwithstanding all this loss of blood,
As from a conduit with ⌜three⌝ issuing spouts,   30
Yet do thy cheeks look red as Titan's face,
Blushing to be encountered with a cloud.
Shall I speak for thee, shall I say 'tis so?
O, that I knew thy heart, and knew the beast,
That I might rail at him to ease my mind.   35
Sorrow concealèd, like an oven stopped,
Doth burn the heart to cinders where it is.
Fair Philomela, why she but lost her tongue,
And in a tedious sampler sewed her mind;
But, lovely niece, that mean is cut from thee.   40
A craftier Tereus, cousin, hast thou met,
And he hath cut those pretty fingers off
That could have better sewed than Philomel.
O, had the monster seen those lily hands
Tremble like aspen leaves upon a lute   45
And make the silken strings delight to kiss them,
He would not then have touched them for his life.
Or had he heard the heavenly harmony
Which that sweet tongue hath made,
He would have dropped his knife and fell asleep,   50
As Cerberus at the Thracian poet's feet.
Come, let us go and make thy father blind,
For such a sight will blind a father's eye.
One hour's storm will drown the fragrant meads;
What will whole months of tears thy father's eyes?   55
Do not draw back, for we will mourn with thee.
O, could our mourning ease thy misery!
                                        They exit.

TITUS
ANDRONICUS

ACT 3

3.1   Martius and Quintus are led off to execution. Aaron says their lives can be saved if Titus, Lucius, or Marcus cuts off a hand and sends it as ransom. Titus sends his hand, and a messenger returns the hand and the heads of Martius and Quintus. Titus vows revenge, telling the exiled Lucius to raise an army of Goths to march on Rome.

---

   4. **quarrel:** cause
   5. **watched:** remained awake intentionally (and on guard against danger to Rome)
   8. **pitiful:** compassionate
   9. **souls is:** i.e., **souls** are
   10. **two-and-twenty sons:** See longer note, page 212.
   11 SD. **lieth down:** i.e., prostrates himself
   13. **languor:** sorrow
   14. **stanch:** allay, satisfy
   15. **shame:** be ashamed
   18. **his:** its

⟨ACT 3⟩

Enter the Judges and Senators with Titus' two sons
(⌈Quintus and Martius⌉) bound, passing on the stage to
the place of execution, and Titus going before, pleading.

TITUS
    Hear me, grave fathers; noble tribunes, stay.
    For pity of mine age, whose youth was spent
    In dangerous wars whilst you securely slept;
    For all my blood in Rome's great quarrel shed,
    For all the frosty nights that I have watched,   5
    And for these bitter tears which now you see,
    Filling the agèd wrinkles in my cheeks,
    Be pitiful to my condemnèd sons,
    Whose souls is not corrupted as 'tis thought.
    For two-and-twenty sons I never wept   10
    Because they died in honor's lofty bed.
       Andronicus lieth down, and the Judges pass by him.
⌈*They exit with the prisoners as Titus continues speaking.*⌉
    For these, tribunes, in the dust I write
    My heart's deep languor and my soul's sad tears.
    Let my tears stanch the earth's dry appetite.
    My sons' sweet blood will make it shame and blush.   15
    O earth, I will befriend thee more with rain
    That shall distil from these two ancient ruins
    Than youthful April shall with all his showers.

19. **still:** continually
22. **So:** provided that
24. **doom:** sentence
26. **orators:** advocates
28. **by:** nearby
34. **mark:** pay attention to
36. **bootless:** in vain
39. **in some sort:** to some extent
40. **For that:** because; **intercept:** interrupt
43. **grave weeds:** sober garments
44. **afford:** provide
48. **doom:** sentence
49. **wherefore:** why

In summer's drought I'll drop upon thee still;
In winter with warm tears I'll melt the snow   20
And keep eternal springtime on thy face,
So thou refuse to drink my dear sons' blood.

Enter Lucius with his weapon drawn.

O reverend tribunes, O gentle agèd men,
Unbind my sons, reverse the doom of death,
And let me say, that never wept before,   25
My tears are now prevailing orators.

LUCIUS
O noble father, you lament in vain.
The Tribunes hear you not; no man is by,
And you recount your sorrows to a stone.

TITUS
Ah, Lucius, for thy brothers let me plead.—   30
Grave tribunes, once more I entreat of you—

LUCIUS
My gracious lord, no tribune hears you speak.

TITUS
Why, 'tis no matter, man. If they did hear,
They would not mark me; if they did mark,
They would not pity me. Yet plead I must,   35
And bootless unto them.
Therefore I tell my sorrows to the stones,
Who, though they cannot answer my distress,
Yet in some sort they are better than the Tribunes,
For that they will not intercept my tale.   40
When I do weep, they humbly at my feet
Receive my tears and seem to weep with me,
And were they but attirèd in grave weeds,
Rome could afford no tribunes like to these.
A stone is soft as wax, tribunes more hard than   45
  stones;
A stone is silent and offendeth not,
And tribunes with their tongues doom men to death.
But wherefore stand'st thou with thy weapon drawn?

57. happy: fortunate

66. object: sight, spectacle

67. arise: Lucius has either collapsed or knelt. He rises at some point during Titus's speech to Lavinia.

70. hath . . . sea: Proverbial: "To cast water into the sea."

71. faggot: bundle of sticks bound up to serve as fuel; **Troy:** burned by the Greeks at the end of the Trojan War (See picture below.)

73. Nilus: the Nile River; **disdaineth bounds:** i.e., overflows (The Nile floods annually.)

Aeneas carrying his father from
"bright-burning Troy." (3.1.71; 3.2.27–28)
From Geoffrey Whitney, *A choice of emblemes* . . . (1586).

LUCIUS
> To rescue my two brothers from their death, 50
> For which attempt the Judges have pronounced
> My everlasting doom of banishment.

TITUS, ⌈*rising*⌉
> O happy man, they have befriended thee!
> Why, foolish Lucius, dost thou not perceive
> That Rome is but a wilderness of tigers? 55
> Tigers must prey, and Rome affords no prey
> But me and mine. How happy art thou then
> From these devourers to be banishèd.
> But who comes with our brother Marcus here?

Enter Marcus with Lavinia.

MARCUS
> Titus, prepare thy agèd eyes to weep, 60
> Or, if not so, thy noble heart to break.
> I bring consuming sorrow to thine age.

TITUS
> Will it consume me? Let me see it, then.

MARCUS
> This was thy daughter.

TITUS   Why, Marcus, so she is. 65

LUCIUS   Ay me, this object kills me!

TITUS
> Faint-hearted boy, arise and look upon her.—
> Speak, Lavinia. What accursèd hand
> Hath made thee handless in thy father's sight?
> What fool hath added water to the sea 70
> Or brought a faggot to bright-burning Troy?
> My grief was at the height before thou cam'st,
> And now like Nilus it disdaineth bounds.—
> Give me a sword. I'll chop off my hands too,
> For they have fought for Rome and all in vain; 75
> And they have nursed this woe in feeding life;

78. **effectless:** fruitless
83. **martyred:** mutilated
84. **engine:** instrument, organ
90. **park:** hunting ground
92. **unrecuring:** incurable
96. **Environed with:** surrounded by
98. **Expecting ever:** i.e., always anticipating the time; **envious:** malicious
99. **his brinish:** its salty; or, perhaps, its seawater
103. **spurn:** contemptuous stroke (literally, a kick)
106. **madded:** maddened
107. **lively:** living

In bootless prayer have they been held up,
And they have served me to effectless use.
Now all the service I require of them
Is that the one will help to cut the other.—   80
'Tis well, Lavinia, that thou hast no hands,
For hands to do Rome service is but vain.

LUCIUS
Speak, gentle sister. Who hath martyred thee?

MARCUS
O, that delightful engine of her thoughts,
That blabbed them with such pleasing eloquence,   85
Is torn from forth that pretty hollow cage
Where, like a sweet melodious bird, it sung
Sweet varied notes, enchanting every ear.

LUCIUS
O, say thou for her who hath done this deed!

MARCUS
O, thus I found her straying in the park,   90
Seeking to hide herself as doth the deer
That hath received some unrecuring wound.

TITUS
It was my dear, and he that wounded her
Hath hurt me more than had he killed me dead.
For now I stand as one upon a rock,   95
Environed with a wilderness of sea,
Who marks the waxing tide grow wave by wave,
Expecting ever when some envious surge
Will in his brinish bowels swallow him.
This way to death my wretched sons are gone;   100
Here stands my other son a banished man,
And here my brother, weeping at my woes.
But that which gives my soul the greatest spurn
Is dear Lavinia, dearer than my soul.
Had I but seen thy picture in this plight   105
It would have madded me. What shall I do,
Now I behold thy lively body so?

111. **by this:** i.e., **by this** time

114. **honeydew:** a sweet sticky substance found on plants, once thought to be a kind of dew

121. **sorrow:** lamentation (*To make sorrow* meant "to express grief or mourning.")

123. **do thee ease:** assist you

125. **fountain:** water springing from the earth and collected in a natural basin

131. **And made:** i.e., **and the fountain be made**

133. **bite:** i.e., **bite** out; **dumb shows:** mimes; scenes composed of action without dialogue (a feature sometimes included in Elizabethan plays)

Thou hast no hands to wipe away thy tears,
Nor tongue to tell me who hath martyred thee.
Thy husband he is dead, and for his death   110
Thy brothers are condemned, and dead by this.—
Look, Marcus!—Ah, son Lucius, look on her!
When I did name her brothers, then fresh tears
Stood on her cheeks as doth the honeydew
Upon a gathered lily almost withered.   115

MARCUS
Perchance she weeps because they killed her husband,
Perchance because she knows them innocent.

TITUS
If they did kill thy husband, then be joyful,
Because the law hath ta'en revenge on them.—
No, no, they would not do so foul a deed.   120
Witness the sorrow that their sister makes.—
Gentle Lavinia, let me kiss thy lips,
Or make some sign how I may do thee ease.
Shall thy good uncle and thy brother Lucius
And thou and I sit round about some fountain,   125
Looking all downwards to behold our cheeks,
How they are stained like meadows yet not dry
With miry slime left on them by a flood?
And in the fountain shall we gaze so long
Till the fresh taste be taken from that clearness   130
And made a brine pit with our bitter tears?
Or shall we cut away our hands like thine?
Or shall we bite our tongues and in dumb shows
Pass the remainder of our hateful days?
What shall we do? Let us that have our tongues   135
Plot some device of further misery
To make us wondered at in time to come.

LUCIUS
Sweet father, cease your tears, for at your grief
See how my wretched sister sobs and weeps.

141. **wot:** know
142. **napkin:** handkerchief
148. **bewet:** profusely wet
150. **sympathy:** harmony, agreement, likeness
151. **limbo:** i.e., hell or Hades; **bliss:** heaven

Orpheus, the Thracian poet. (2.4.51)
From Ovid, . . . *Metamorphoseon* . . . (1565).

MARCUS
    Patience, dear niece.—Good Titus, dry thine eyes.   140
TITUS
    Ah, Marcus, Marcus! Brother, well I wot
    Thy napkin cannot drink a tear of mine,
    For thou, poor man, hast drowned it with thine own.
LUCIUS
    Ah, my Lavinia, I will wipe thy cheeks.
TITUS
    Mark, Marcus, mark. I understand her signs.   145
    Had she a tongue to speak, now would she say
    That to her brother which I said to thee.
    His napkin, with ⌈his⌉ true tears all bewet,
    Can do no service on her sorrowful cheeks.
    O, what a sympathy of woe is this,   150
    As far from help as limbo is from bliss.

                Enter Aaron the Moor alone.

AARON
    Titus Andronicus, my lord the Emperor
    Sends thee this word, that if thou love thy sons,
    Let Marcus, Lucius, or thyself, old Titus,
    Or any one of you, chop off your hand   155
    And send it to the King; he for the same
    Will send thee hither both thy sons alive,
    And that shall be the ransom for their fault.
TITUS
    O gracious emperor! O gentle Aaron!
    Did ever raven sing so like a lark,   160
    That gives sweet tidings of the sun's uprise?
    With all my heart I'll send the Emperor my hand.
    Good Aaron, wilt thou help to chop it off?
LUCIUS
    Stay, father, for that noble hand of thine,
    That hath thrown down so many enemies,   165
    Shall not be sent. My hand will serve the turn.

172. **none of both but:** i.e., **both**
175. **to a worthy end:** i.e., for **a worthy** purpose
181. **meet:** appropriate
182. **shall:** i.e., am to

Aeneas and Dido. (2.3.22; 3.2.27–28)
From [Guillaume Rouillé,] . . . *Promptuarii iconum* . . . (1553).

My youth can better spare my blood than you,
And therefore mine shall save my brothers' lives.

MARCUS
Which of your hands hath not defended Rome
And reared aloft the bloody battleax,   170
Writing destruction on the enemy's castle?
O, none of both but are of high desert.
My hand hath been but idle; let it serve
To ransom my two nephews from their death.
Then have I kept it to a worthy end.   175

AARON
Nay, come, agree whose hand shall go along,
For fear they die before their pardon come.

MARCUS
My hand shall go.

LUCIUS   By heaven, it shall not go!

TITUS
Sirs, strive no more. Such withered herbs as these   180
Are meet for plucking up, and therefore mine.

LUCIUS
Sweet father, if I shall be thought thy son,
Let me redeem my brothers both from death.

MARCUS
And for our father's sake and mother's care,
Now let me show a brother's love to thee.   185

TITUS
Agree between you. I will spare my hand.

LUCIUS   Then I'll go fetch an ax.

MARCUS   But I will use the ax. ⌜*Lucius and Marcus*⌝ *exit.*

TITUS
Come hither, Aaron. I'll deceive them both.
Lend me thy hand, and I will give thee mine.   190

AARON, ⌜*aside*⌝
If that be called deceit, I will be honest
And never whilst I live deceive men so.

193. **sort:** way
195. **stay:** stop; **dispatched:** concluded
197. **warded:** protected, guarded
200. **account of:** account, value
202. **dear:** expensive
204. **by and by:** soon
206. **fat:** fatten; i.e., delight
207. **fair men:** i.e., **men** of light complexion (also, perhaps **men** free of moral blemish or free of injustice or bias)
210. **this feeble ruin:** i.e., his now mutilated body
216. **breathe the welkin dim:** i.e., make the sky misty or hazy with our breath
217. **stain:** eclipse, obscure; **sometime:** sometimes
219. **with possibility:** i.e., of what is possible
220. **deep:** profound

But I'll deceive you in another sort,
And that you'll say ere half an hour pass.
                              He cuts off Titus' hand.

          Enter Lucius and Marcus again.

TITUS
    Now stay your strife. What shall be is dispatched.—   195
    Good Aaron, give his Majesty my hand.
    Tell him it was a hand that warded him
    From thousand dangers. Bid him bury it.
    More hath it merited; that let it have.
    As for my sons, say I account of them   200
    As jewels purchased at an easy price,
    And yet dear, too, because I bought mine own.
AARON
    I go, Andronicus, and for thy hand
    Look by and by to have thy sons with thee.
    ⌜*Aside.*⌝ Their heads, I mean. O, how this villainy   205
    Doth fat me with the very thoughts of it!
    Let fools do good and fair men call for grace;
    Aaron will have his soul black like his face.
                                        He exits.

TITUS
    O, here I lift this one hand up to heaven,
    And bow this feeble ruin to the earth. ⌜*He kneels.*⌝   210
    If any power pities wretched tears,
    To that I call. (⌜*Lavinia kneels.*⌝) What, wouldst thou
        kneel with me?
    Do, then, dear heart, for heaven shall hear our
        prayers,   215
    Or with our sighs we'll breathe the welkin dim
    And stain the sun with fog, as sometime clouds
    When they do hug him in their melting bosoms.
MARCUS
    O brother, speak with possibility,
    And do not break into these deep extremes.   220

222. **passions:** outbursts; **them:** i.e., my sorrows

225. **bind:** confine

229. **coil:** turmoil

230. **her:** i.e., Lavinia's

235. **Forwhy:** because; **bowels:** wordplay on the physical intestines and the word's figurative use as the seat of compassion

237–38. **losers . . . tongues:** Proverbial: **"Give losers leave** to speak." **stomachs:** feelings; spite, vexation

243. **their sports:** i.e., the amusement of the Emperor and his entourage

244. **That:** i.e., so much so **that**

246. **Etna:** Sicilian volcano (See picture below.)

Mount Etna. (3.1.246)
From Gabriel Rollenhagen, *Nucleus emblematum selectissimorum . . .* (1611).

TITUS
   Is not my sorrow deep, having no bottom?
   Then be my passions bottomless with them.
MARCUS
   But yet let reason govern thy lament.
TITUS
   If there were reason for these miseries,
   Then into limits could I bind my woes.   225
   When heaven doth weep, doth not the earth o'erflow?
   If the winds rage, doth not the sea wax mad,
   Threat'ning the welkin with his big-swoll'n face?
   And wilt thou have a reason for this coil?
   I am the sea. Hark how her sighs doth flow!   230
   She is the weeping welkin, I the earth.
   Then must my sea be movèd with her sighs;
   Then must my earth with her continual tears
   Become a deluge, overflowed and drowned,
   Forwhy my bowels cannot hide her woes   235
   But like a drunkard must I vomit them.
   Then give me leave, for losers will have leave
   To ease their stomachs with their bitter tongues.

   Enter a Messenger with two heads and a hand.

MESSENGER
   Worthy Andronicus, ill art thou repaid
   For that good hand thou sent'st the Emperor.   240
   Here are the heads of thy two noble sons,
   And here's thy hand in scorn to thee sent back.
   Thy grief their sports, thy resolution mocked,
   That woe is me to think upon thy woes
   More than remembrance of my father's death.   245
                                          ⌜*He exits.*⌝

MARCUS
   Now let hot Etna cool in Sicily,
   And be my heart an everburning hell!

249. **To weep . . . some deal:** See Romans 12.15: **"weep with them that weep."** **some deal:** somewhat

250. **flouted at:** mocked, jeered at

252. **shrink:** withdraw

253. **bear his name:** i.e., carry the **name** of **life**

256. **starvèd snake: snake** numb with cold

257. **fearful:** dreadful, terrible

261. **dear:** dire, grievous

264. **control:** repress, overmaster

265. **Rent:** rend

266. **dismal:** calamitous

268. **still:** silent

270. **fits not with:** i.e., is not appropriate to

274. **tributary tears:** i.e., **tears** shed as if as tribute paid to the conqueror **sorrow**

These miseries are more than may be borne.
To weep with them that weep doth ease some deal,
But sorrow flouted at is double death.   250

LUCIUS
Ah, that this sight should make so deep a wound
And yet detested life not shrink thereat!
That ever death should let life bear his name,
Where life hath no more interest but to breathe.
                        ⌐*Lavinia kisses Titus.*⌐

MARCUS
Alas, poor heart, that kiss is comfortless   255
As frozen water to a starvèd snake.

TITUS
When will this fearful slumber have an end?

MARCUS
Now farewell, flatt'ry; die, Andronicus.
Thou dost not slumber. See thy two sons' heads,
Thy warlike hand, thy mangled daughter here,   260
Thy other banished son with this dear sight
Struck pale and bloodless; and thy brother, I,
Even like a stony image cold and numb.
Ah, now no more will I control thy griefs.
Rent off thy silver hair, thy other hand,   265
Gnawing with thy teeth, and be this dismal sight
The closing up of our most wretched eyes.
Now is a time to storm. Why art thou still?

TITUS   Ha, ha, ha!

MARCUS
Why dost thou laugh? It fits not with this hour.   270
                        ⌐*Titus and Lavinia rise.*⌐

TITUS
Why, I have not another tear to shed.
Besides, this sorrow is an enemy
And would usurp upon my wat'ry eyes
And make them blind with tributary tears.

277. **threat:** threaten
278. **mischiefs:** evils
281. **heavy:** sorrowful
282–83. **turn . . . wrongs:** The other characters probably stand in a circle around Titus, who in gesture pledges each of them.
286. **these arms:** i.e., this violent revenge
291. **Hie:** hurry
297. **pledges:** perhaps, vows; or, perhaps, family members left behind like hostages
299. **tofore:** formerly
300. **nor . . . nor:** i.e., neither . . . nor
302. **requite:** avenge
304. **Tarquin:** i.e., Lucius Tarquinius Superbus, the last king of Rome, exiled when his son (Sextus Tarquinius, also called **Tarquin** by Shakespeare) raped the chaste Roman matron Lucretia (See note to **Lucrece** at 2.1.115, and pictures, pages 72 and 140.)
305. **a power:** an army

Then which way shall I find Revenge's cave?   275
For these two heads do seem to speak to me
And threat me I shall never come to bliss
Till all these mischiefs be returned again
Even in their throats that hath committed them.
Come, let me see what task I have to do.   280
You heavy people, circle me about
That I may turn me to each one of you
And swear unto my soul to right your wrongs.
The vow is made. Come, brother, take a head,
And in this hand the other will I bear.—   285
And, Lavinia, thou shalt be employed in these arms.
Bear thou my hand, sweet wench, between thy
    teeth.—
As for thee, boy, go get thee from my sight.
Thou art an exile, and thou must not stay.   290
Hie to the Goths and raise an army there.
And if you love me, as I think you do,
Let's kiss and part, for we have much to do.
                              All ⟨but Lucius⟩ exit.

LUCIUS
Farewell, Andronicus, my noble father,
The woefull'st man that ever lived in Rome.   295
Farewell, proud Rome, till Lucius come again.
He loves his pledges dearer than his life.
Farewell, Lavinia, my noble sister.
O, would thou wert as thou tofore hast been!
But now nor Lucius nor Lavinia lives   300
But in oblivion and hateful griefs.
If Lucius live he will requite your wrongs
And make proud Saturnine and his empress
Beg at the gates like Tarquin and his queen.
Now will I to the Goths and raise a power   305
To be revenged on Rome and Saturnine.
                              Lucius exits.

3.2 In this scene, which is found in the 1623 Folio text but not in the Quarto, Titus is horrified when Marcus kills an innocent fly, but then turns on the dead fly in rage when told that it resembles Aaron the Moor.

---

0 SD. **A banquet:** perhaps, a feast; perhaps, a course of fruit and wine

1. **look:** make sure, take care

4. **unknit ... knot:** unfold your arms (Folded arms signified melancholy.)

5. **want:** lack

6. **passionate:** express or perform with passion

9. **Who:** i.e., which

12. **map:** very picture or image

15. **Wound it with sighing:** a reference to the belief that sighs drew vital blood from the heart

17. **against:** in front of

19. **sink:** pit, pool

23. **made thee dote:** turned you senile

26. **wherefore:** why

27–28. **To bid Aeneas ... miserable:** In the second book of Virgil's *Aeneid*, when Queen Dido asks Aeneas to narrate his adventures, Aeneas replies: "Unspeakable, queen, is the grief you bid me revive." (See picture, page 94.)

29. **handle not:** do not discuss

⌐Scene 2⌐

⟨*A banquet. Enter* ⌐*Titus*⌐ *Andronicus, Marcus, Lavinia,*
and the boy ⌐*Young Lucius, with Servants.*⌐

TITUS
　So, so. Now sit, and look you eat no more
　Than will preserve just so much strength in us
　As will revenge these bitter woes of ours.
　Marcus, unknit that sorrow-wreathen knot.
　Thy niece and I, poor creatures, want our hands   5
　And cannot passionate our tenfold grief
　With folded arms. This poor right hand of mine
　Is left to tyrannize upon my breast,
　Who, when my heart, all mad with misery,
　Beats in this hollow prison of my flesh,   10
　Then thus I thump it down.—
　Thou map of woe, that thus dost talk in signs,
　When thy poor heart beats with outrageous beating,
　Thou canst not strike it thus to make it still.
　Wound it with sighing, girl, kill it with groans;   15
　Or get some little knife between thy teeth
　And just against thy heart make thou a hole,
　That all the tears that thy poor eyes let fall
　May run into that sink and, soaking in,
　Drown the lamenting fool in sea-salt tears.   20
MARCUS
　Fie, brother, fie! Teach her not thus to lay
　Such violent hands upon her tender life.
TITUS
　How now! Has sorrow made thee dote already?
　Why, Marcus, no man should be mad but I.
　What violent hands can she lay on her life?   25
　Ah, wherefore dost thou urge the name of hands,
　To bid Aeneas tell the tale twice o'er
　How Troy was burnt and he made miserable?
　O, handle not the theme, to talk of hands,

30. **still:** now
31. **square:** shape
38. **with:** by; **mashed:** mixed, mingled (with wordplay on "crushed to mash in preparation for brewing")
40. **dumb action:** i.e., speechless communication; **perfect:** "To be **perfect in**" means "to be thoroughly versed or skilled in."
43. **wink:** close your eyes
44. **of:** i.e., from
45. **still:** constant
48. **passion:** feeling
49. **heaviness:** grief
54. **Out on thee:** a phrase expressing abhorrence or reproach
55. **tyranny:** violence, outrage
57. **Becomes not:** is not fitting for

Lest we remember still that we have none.—   30
Fie, fie, how franticly I square my talk,
As if we should forget we had no hands
If Marcus did not name the word of hands!
Come, let's fall to, and, gentle girl, eat this.
Here is no drink!—Hark, Marcus, what she says.   35
I can interpret all her martyred signs.
She says she drinks no other drink but tears
Brewed with her sorrow, mashed upon her cheeks.—
Speechless complainer, I will learn thy thought.
In thy dumb action will I be as perfect   40
As begging hermits in their holy prayers.
Thou shalt not sigh, nor hold thy stumps to heaven,
Nor wink, nor nod, nor kneel, nor make a sign,
But I of these will wrest an alphabet
And by still practice learn to know thy meaning.   45

YOUNG LUCIUS, ⌜*weeping*⌝
Good grandsire, leave these bitter deep laments.
Make my aunt merry with some pleasing tale.

MARCUS
Alas, the tender boy, in passion moved,
Doth weep to see his grandsire's heaviness.

TITUS
Peace, tender sapling. Thou art made of tears,   50
And tears will quickly melt thy life away.
                    Marcus strikes the dish with a knife.
What dost thou strike at, Marcus, with ⌜thy⌝ knife?

MARCUS
At that that I have killed, my lord, a fly.

TITUS
Out on thee, murderer! Thou kill'st my heart.
Mine eyes ⌜are⌝ cloyed with view of tyranny;   55
A deed of death done on the innocent
Becomes not Titus' brother. Get thee gone.
I see thou art not for my company.

59. **but:** merely

61. **he:** i.e., the fly's **father** (line 60)

62. **lamenting doings:** perhaps, lamentations

67. **ill-favored:** ugly

72. **insult on:** exult proudly over, triumph over

73. **Flattering:** gratifying

75. **There's . . . that's:** These words accompany Titus's stabbing at the fly.

80. **wrought:** worked

81. **false:** deceptive; **shadows:** semblances, symbols or signs

82. **take away:** i.e., clear the banquet

83. **closet:** private room

84. **chancèd:** i.e., that happened

86. **mine:** i.e., my eyes; **dazzle:** blur (perhaps with tears)

MARCUS
  Alas, my lord, I have but killed a fly.
TITUS
  "But"? How if that fly had a father and mother?   60
  How would he hang his slender gilded wings
  And buzz lamenting doings in the air!
  Poor harmless fly,
  That, with his pretty buzzing melody,
  Came here to make us merry! And thou hast killed   65
    him.
MARCUS
  Pardon me, sir. It was a black, ill-favored fly,
  Like to the Empress' Moor. Therefore I killed him.
TITUS   O, O, O!
  Then pardon me for reprehending thee,   70
  For thou hast done a charitable deed.
  Give me thy knife. I will insult on him,
  Flattering myself as if it were the Moor
  Come hither purposely to poison me.
  There's for thyself, and that's for Tamora.   75
  Ah, sirrah!
  Yet I think we are not brought so low
  But that between us we can kill a fly
  That comes in likeness of a coalblack Moor.
MARCUS
  Alas, poor man, grief has so wrought on him   80
  He takes false shadows for true substances.
TITUS
  Come, take away.—Lavinia, go with me.
  I'll to thy closet and go read with thee
  Sad stories chancèd in the times of old.—
  Come, boy, and go with me. Thy sight is young,   85
  And thou shalt read when mine begin to dazzle.
                                  They exit.⟩

TITUS
ANDRONICUS

ACT 4

4.1 Lavinia finds a way to reveal to Titus the story of her rape and mutilation and the names of the rapists.

---

1. **grandsire:** grandfather
9. **Somewhat:** something
11. **Somewhither:** somewhere
12. **Cornelia:** daughter of Scipio Africanus Major and the ideal Roman mother, whose sons the Gracchi became famous tribunes (2nd century B.C.E.)
14. **Tully's Orator:** either *De Oratore* or *Orator,* both treatises by Marcus Tullius Cicero (106–43 B.C.E.) See picture below.

Title page of Cicero's *De Oratore* (1573). (4.1.14)
(The scribbles suggest a schoolboy's copy.)

⟨ACT 4⟩

⌜Scene 1⌝

*Enter Lucius' son and Lavinia running after him, and
the boy flies from her with his books under his arm.
Enter Titus and Marcus.*

YOUNG LUCIUS
  Help, grandsire, help! My aunt Lavinia
  Follows me everywhere, I know not why.—
  Good uncle Marcus, see how swift she comes!—
  Alas, sweet aunt, I know not what you mean.

MARCUS
  Stand by me, Lucius. Do not fear thine aunt.   5

TITUS
  She loves thee, boy, too well to do thee harm.

YOUNG LUCIUS
  Ay, when my father was in Rome she did.

MARCUS
  What means my niece Lavinia by these signs?

TITUS
  Fear her not, Lucius. Somewhat doth she mean.
  See, Lucius, see, how much she makes of thee.   10
  Somewhither would she have thee go with her.
  ⌜Ah,⌝ boy, Cornelia never with more care
  Read to her sons than she hath read to thee
  Sweet poetry and Tully's *Orator.*

121

15. **wherefore:** why; **plies thee:** persistently solicits you

18. **full oft:** very often

20. **Hecuba of Troy:** See note to 1.1.136–38. (**Hecuba** went mad after avenging herself on Polymnestor.)

24. **fury:** disorder of the mind approaching madness

28. **attend:** accompany

33–34. **better skilled:** more knowledgeable or experienced

36. **beguile:** charm away, divert or distract

40. **fact:** crime

43. **Ovid's Metamorphosis:** Although the title of Ovid's work is today written *Metamorphoses*, we retain the Quarto spelling, since it follows the title as it appeared in the sixteenth century. (See picture, page 184.) For the relevant part of this text, see Appendix.

King Priam. (1.1.80)

From [Guillaume Rouillé,] . . . *Promptuarii iconum* . . . (1553).

⌈MARCUS⌉
  Canst thou not guess wherefore she plies thee thus? 15
YOUNG LUCIUS
  My lord, I know not, I, nor can I guess,
  Unless some fit or frenzy do possess her;
  For I have heard my grandsire say full oft,
  Extremity of griefs would make men mad,
  And I have read that Hecuba of Troy 20
  Ran mad for sorrow. That made me to fear,
  Although, my lord, I know my noble aunt
  Loves me as dear as e'er my mother did,
  And would not but in fury fright my youth,
  Which made me down to throw my books and fly, 25
  Causeless, perhaps.—But pardon me, sweet aunt.
  And, madam, if my uncle Marcus go,
  I will most willingly attend your Ladyship.
MARCUS   Lucius, I will.
TITUS
  How now, Lavinia?—Marcus, what means this? 30
  Some book there is that she desires to see.—
  Which is it, girl, of these?—Open them, boy.—
  ⌈*To Lavinia.*⌉ But thou art deeper read and better
    skilled.
  Come and take choice of all my library, 35
  And so beguile thy sorrow till the heavens
  Reveal the damned contriver of this deed.—
  Why lifts she up her arms in sequence thus?
MARCUS
  I think she means that there were more than one
  Confederate in the fact. Ay, more there was, 40
  Or else to heaven she heaves them for revenge.
TITUS
  Lucius, what book is that she tosseth so?
YOUNG LUCIUS
  Grandsire, 'tis Ovid's *Metamorphosis*.
  My mother gave it me.

47. **Soft:** i.e., wait a minute

49–50. **Philomel . . . rape:** See notes to 2.3.43 and 2.4.38–39.

51. **annoy:** molestation

52. **quotes:** scrutinizes

53. **surprised:** attacked suddenly and without warning

55. **vast:** waste, uninhabited, deserted

58. **Patterned:** prefigured (Ovid describes the site of Philomela's rape as "a pelting grange [paltry country house] that peakishly [steep-roofed] did stand / In woods forgrown [overgrown]" [*Metamorphosis*, trans. Golding, 6.663–64].)

62. **friends:** relatives

64. **Tarquin:** See note to **Lucrece** at 2.1.115 and to **Tarquin** at 3.1.304. (See picture, page 140.)

65. **camp:** i.e., the Roman military **camp,** which **Tarquin** left when he set off to rape Lucrece

67. **Apollo:** god of the sun and of prophecy; also associated with moral law and music (See picture, page 202.) **Pallas:** i.e., **Pallas** Athena, goddess of wisdom, law, and order; **Jove:** i.e., Jupiter, king and therefore judge of the gods; **Mercury:** god who serves as Jupiter's messenger (See picture, page 130.)

68. **treason:** treacherous action, treachery

70. **plot:** spot; **plain:** smooth

MARCUS For love of her that's gone,   45
  Perhaps, she culled it from among the rest.
TITUS
  Soft! So busily she turns the leaves.
  Help her! What would she find?—Lavinia, shall I read?
  This is the tragic tale of Philomel,
  And treats of Tereus' treason and his rape.   50
  And rape, I fear, was root of thy annoy.
MARCUS
  See, brother, see! Note how she quotes the leaves.
TITUS
  Lavinia, wert thou thus surprised, sweet girl,
  Ravished and wronged as Philomela was,
  Forced in the ruthless, vast, and gloomy woods?   55
  See, see! Ay, such a place there is where we did hunt—
  O, had we never, never hunted there!—
  Patterned by that the poet here describes,
  By nature made for murders and for rapes.
MARCUS
  O, why should nature build so foul a den,   60
  Unless the gods delight in tragedies?
TITUS
  Give signs, sweet girl, for here are none but friends,
  What Roman lord it was durst do the deed.
  Or slunk not Saturnine, as Tarquin erst,
  That left the camp to sin in Lucrece' bed?   65
MARCUS
  Sit down, sweet niece.—Brother, sit down by me.
                                          ⌜*They sit.*⌝

  Apollo, Pallas, Jove, or Mercury
  Inspire me, that I may this treason find.—
  My lord, look here.—Look here, Lavinia.
          He writes his name with his staff and guides it
                                    with feet and mouth.
  This sandy plot is plain; guide, if thou canst,   70
  This after me. I have writ my name

73. **shift:** contrivance; extremity

75. **will have discovered for revenge:** i.e., desires to be revealed so that it can be avenged

79. **Stuprum:** rape (Latin)

82–83. **Magni . . . vides:** Ruler of the great heavens, do you so calmly hear and see crimes (an adaptation of Seneca's *Hippolytus*, lines 671–72).

87. **exclaims:** exclamations, outcries

89. **Roman Hector's:** i.e., Lucius's (Hector was the greatest of the Trojan warriors. See picture below.) **hope:** person in whom hopes are centered

90–92. **as . . . rape:** i.e., **as Junius Brutus** joined Lucrece's father and husband in vowing to avenge her **rape** (**Junius Brutus** led the rebellion against King Tarquin and founded the Roman Republic. See also notes to 2.1.115 and 3.1.304.) **fere:** husband

93. **by good advice:** i.e., according to a **good** plan

95. **reproach:** disgrace; insult

96. **an:** if

98. **dam:** i.e., mother bear; **an if she wind:** i.e., **if she** get wind of

Hector. (4.1.89)
From [Guillaume Rouillé,] . . . *Promptuarii iconum* . . . (1553).

Without the help of any hand at all.
Cursed be that heart that forced us to this shift!
Write thou, good niece, and here display at last
What God will have discovered for revenge.   75
Heaven guide thy pen to print thy sorrows plain,
That we may know the traitors and the truth.

> *She takes the staff in her mouth, and guides it*
> *with her stumps and writes.*

O, do you read, my lord, what she hath writ?

⌈TITUS⌉
"*Stuprum.* Chiron, Demetrius."

MARCUS
What, what! The lustful sons of Tamora   80
Performers of this heinous, bloody deed?

TITUS *Magni Dominator poli,*
Tam lentus audis scelera, tam lentus vides?

MARCUS
O, calm thee, gentle lord, although I know
There is enough written upon this earth   85
To stir a mutiny in the mildest thoughts
And arm the minds of infants to exclaims.
My lord, kneel down with me.—Lavinia, kneel.—
And kneel, sweet boy, the Roman Hector's hope,

> ⌈*They all kneel.*⌉

And swear with me—as, with the woeful fere   90
And father of that chaste dishonored dame,
Lord Junius Brutus swore for Lucrece' rape—
That we will prosecute by good advice
Mortal revenge upon these traitorous Goths,
And see their blood or die with this reproach.   95

> ⌈*They rise.*⌉

TITUS
'Tis sure enough, an you knew how.
But if you hunt these bearwhelps, then beware;
The dam will wake an if she wind you once.
She's with the lion deeply still in league,

101. **list:** likes, wishes

102. **young:** inexperienced, unpracticed; **let alone:** i.e., let it **alone**

103. **leaf:** sheet

104. **gad:** i.e., stylus

106. **Sibyl's leaves:** i.e., the **leaves** on which the Sibyl of Cumae wrote her prophecies (See picture below.)

109. **Their mother's:** i.e., even **their mother's**

111. **full oft:** very often

115. **fit thee:** i.e., provide for you what you need; **withal:** i.e., in addition

122. **brave it:** swagger

123. **marry:** indeed (originally, an oath on the name of the Virgin Mary, and thus an anachronism in this play); **waited on:** gazed at

125. **compassion:** pity

126. **attend:** watch over; **ecstasy:** frenzy

The Cumaean Sibyl. (4.1.106)
From Philippus de Barberiis, *Quattuor hic compressa opuscula . . .* (ca. 1495).

128

And lulls him whilst she playeth on her back;   100
And when he sleeps will she do what she list.
You are a young huntsman, Marcus; let alone.
And come, I will go get a leaf of brass,
And with a gad of steel will write these words,
And lay it by. The angry northern wind   105
Will blow these sands like Sibyl's leaves abroad,
And where's our lesson then?—Boy, what say you?

YOUNG LUCIUS
  I say, my lord, that if I were a man,
  Their mother's bedchamber should not be safe
  For these base bondmen to the yoke of Rome.   110

MARCUS
  Ay, that's my boy! Thy father hath full oft
  For his ungrateful country done the like.

YOUNG LUCIUS
  And, uncle, so will I, an if I live.

TITUS
  Come, go with me into mine armory.
  Lucius, I'll fit thee, and withal my boy   115
  Shall carry from me to the Empress' sons
  Presents that I intend to send them both.
  Come, come. Thou'lt do my message, wilt thou not?

YOUNG LUCIUS
  Ay, with my dagger in their bosoms, grandsire.

TITUS
  No, boy, not so. I'll teach thee another course.—   120
  Lavinia, come.—Marcus, look to my house.
  Lucius and I'll go brave it at the court;
  Ay, marry, will we, sir, and we'll be waited on.
                All ⌜*but Marcus*⌝ *exit.*

MARCUS
  O heavens, can you hear a good man groan
  And not relent, or not compassion him?   125
  Marcus, attend him in his ecstasy,
  That hath more scars of sorrow in his heart

128. **foemen's:** enemies'
130. **Revenge . . . for:** i.e., let **the heavens** avenge

4.2 Tamora gives birth to a baby whose black skin signals Aaron's paternity. Aaron arranges for a white baby to take his son's place as Saturninus's heir. He then sets out to take his baby to safety among the Goths.

---

6. **confound:** destroy
7. **Gramercy:** thanks
8. **deciphered:** detected, found out
10. **well advised:** after due consideration
11. **goodliest:** most excellent
12. **gratify:** make a present to; please
16. **appointed:** equipped

Mercury. (4.1.67; 4.3.57)
From Giovanni Battista Cavalleriis,
Antiquarum statuarum . . . (1585–94).

Than foemen's marks upon his battered shield,
But yet so just that he will not revenge.
Revenge the heavens for old Andronicus!   130

He exits.

⌜Scene 2⌝

*Enter Aaron, Chiron, and Demetrius at one door, and at
the other door young Lucius and another, with a bundle
of weapons and verses writ upon them.*

CHIRON
Demetrius, here's the son of Lucius.
He hath some message to deliver us.

AARON
Ay, some mad message from his mad grandfather.

YOUNG LUCIUS
My lords, with all the humbleness I may,
I greet your Honors from Andronicus—   5
⌜*Aside.*⌝ And pray the Roman gods confound you both.

DEMETRIUS
Gramercy, lovely Lucius. What's the news?

YOUNG LUCIUS, ⌜*aside*⌝
That you are both deciphered, that's the news,
For villains marked with rape.—May it please you,
My grandsire, well advised, hath sent by me   10
The goodliest weapons of his armory
To gratify your honorable youth,
The hope of Rome; for so he bid me say,
And so I do, and with his gifts present
Your Lordships, ⌜that,⌝ whenever you have need,   15
You may be armèd and appointed well,
And so I leave you both—(⌜*aside*⌝) like bloody villains.
                    He exits, ⌜*with Attendant.*⌝

DEMETRIUS
What's here? A scroll, and written round about.

20–21. **Integer ... arcu:** He who is of upright life and free of crime does not need the javelins or bow of the Moor (Horace's *Odes* 1.22.1–2).

23. **the grammar:** William Lily's standard Latin **grammar** twice quotes these lines from Horace. (See picture, page 204.)

24. **just:** precisely

26. **no sound jest: no** good joke (said ironically)

29. **feeling:** i.e., capacity to feel

30. **witty:** clever; **afoot:** i.e., on her feet (We learn soon that Tamora is in the process of giving birth.)

31. **conceit:** device, conception

32. **rest:** wordplay on (1) remain; (2) lie down

33. **happy:** fortunate

37. **brave:** defy; **the tribune:** i.e., Marcus

39. **insinuate:** ingratiate himself

42. **would:** wish

43. **At such a bay:** so cornered or trapped (like a hunted animal surrounded by hounds) (See picture, page 182.)

Let's see:
⌐*He reads:*⌐ "*Integer vitae, scelerisque purus,*   20
          Non eget Mauri iaculis, nec arcu."

CHIRON

O, 'tis a verse in Horace; I know it well.
I read it in the grammar long ago.

AARON

Ay, just; a verse in Horace; right, you have it.
⌐*Aside.*⌐ Now, what a thing it is to be an ass!   25
Here's no sound jest. The old man hath found their
     guilt
And sends them weapons wrapped about with lines
That wound, beyond their feeling, to the quick.
But were our witty empress well afoot,   30
She would applaud Andronicus' conceit.
But let her rest in her unrest awhile.—
And now, young lords, was 't not a happy star
Led us to Rome, strangers, and, more than so,
Captives, to be advancèd to this height?   35
It did me good before the palace gate
To brave the tribune in his brother's hearing.

DEMETRIUS

But me more good to see so great a lord
Basely insinuate and send us gifts.

AARON

Had he not reason, Lord Demetrius?   40
Did you not use his daughter very friendly?

DEMETRIUS

I would we had a thousand Roman dames
At such a bay, by turn to serve our lust.

CHIRON

A charitable wish, and full of love!

AARON

Here lacks but your mother for to say amen.   45

CHIRON

And that would she, for twenty thousand more.

48. **pains:** i.e., **pains** of childbirth

50. **flourish:** sound a fanfare

51. **Belike:** probably

52. **Soft:** wait

53. **morrow:** morning

55. **more:** punning on **Moor** (line 54); **ne'er . . . all:** not **at all** (perhaps, with wordplay on **whit** as "white")

56. **what:** i.e., **what** do you want

57. **gentle:** a polite or ingratiating term of address; **undone:** ruined

60. **fumble:** wrap up clumsily

65. **brought abed:** delivered of a child (Aaron's initial response plays on the meaning "put in bed.")

68. **dam:** mother; **issue:** outcome (with wordplay picked up in line 69)

DEMETRIUS
   Come, let us go and pray to all the gods
   For our belovèd mother in her pains.
AARON, ⌜*aside*⌝
   Pray to the devils; the gods have given us over.
                           ⌜ *Trumpets sound* ⌜*offstage.*⌝

DEMETRIUS
   Why do the Emperor's trumpets flourish thus?   50
CHIRON
   Belike for joy the Emperor hath a son.
DEMETRIUS   Soft, who comes here?

Enter Nurse, with a blackamoor child ⌜*in her arms.*⌝

NURSE   Good morrow, lords.
   O, tell me, did you see Aaron the Moor?
AARON
   Well, more or less, or ne'er a whit at all,   55
   Here Aaron is. And what with Aaron now?
NURSE
   O, gentle Aaron, we are all undone!
   Now help, or woe betide thee evermore.
AARON
   Why, what a caterwauling dost thou keep!
   What dost thou wrap and fumble in thy arms?   60
NURSE
   O, that which I would hide from heaven's eye,
   Our empress' shame and stately Rome's disgrace.
   She is delivered, lords, she is delivered.
AARON   To whom?
NURSE   I mean, she is brought abed.   65
AARON
   Well, God give her good rest. What hath he sent her?
NURSE   A devil.
AARON
   Why, then she is the devil's dam. A joyful issue!

69. **issue:** i.e., child

71. **fair-faced:** light-complexioned

72. **thy stamp, thy seal:** i.e., imprinted with a **stamp** or **seal** confirming your ownership (or, here, paternity)

74. **Zounds:** by God's wounds (a very strong oath)

75. **blowse:** literally, a fat red-faced wench

80. **have done: have** copulated with

82. **chance:** luck

82, 83. **damned, Accursed:** i.e., be **damned,** be **accursed**

89. **broach:** impale

91. **bowels:** intestines

92. **Stay:** stop

94. **got:** begotten, conceived

97. **younglings:** youngsters; **Enceladus:** one of the mythological giants who warred on the gods (so huge and powerful that only burial beneath Mount Etna could keep him down)

Mars, the "god of war." (4.2.99; 4.3.56)
From Vincenzo Cartari, *Le imagini de i dei de gli antichi* . . . (1587).

NURSE
A joyless, dismal, black, and sorrowful issue!
Here is the babe, as loathsome as a toad   70
Amongst the fair-faced breeders of our clime.
The Empress sends it thee, thy stamp, thy seal,
And bids thee christen it with thy dagger's point.

AARON
Zounds, you whore, is black so base a hue?
⌜*To the baby.*⌝ Sweet blowse, you are a beauteous   75
blossom, sure.

DEMETRIUS   Villain, what hast thou done?

AARON   That which thou canst not undo.

CHIRON   Thou hast undone our mother.

AARON   Villain, I have done thy mother.   80

DEMETRIUS
And therein, hellish dog, thou hast undone her.
Woe to her chance, and damned her loathèd choice!
Accursed the offspring of so foul a fiend!

CHIRON   It shall not live.

AARON   It shall not die.   85

NURSE
Aaron, it must. The mother wills it so.

AARON
What, must it, nurse? Then let no man but I
Do execution on my flesh and blood.

DEMETRIUS
I'll broach the tadpole on my rapier's point.
Nurse, give it me. My sword shall soon dispatch it.   90

AARON, ⌜*taking the baby*⌝
Sooner this sword shall plow thy bowels up!
Stay, murderous villains, will you kill your brother?
Now, by the burning tapers of the sky
That shone so brightly when this boy was got,
He dies upon my scimitar's sharp point   95
That touches this my firstborn son and heir.
I tell you, younglings, not Enceladus

98. **Typhon's brood:** Typhon was a mythological fire-breathing, hundred-headed monster who fathered the winds and, perhaps, the Harpies, wind-spirits with women's faces and birds' bodies.

99. **Alcides:** Hercules, the mortal son of Zeus, legendary for his strength (See picture, page 164.) **the god of war:** Mars (See picture, page 136.)

101. **sanguine:** red-faced; **shallow-hearted:** cowardly

102. **white-limed:** whitewashed; **alehouse painted signs:** i.e., crudely painted signboards

105. **For:** because

105–7. **all ... flood:** proverbial **she:** i.e., **the ocean lave:** wash **flood:** tide

114. **maugre:** despite

115. **smoke:** suffer severely

117. **escape:** transgression

118. **doom her death:** i.e., sentence **her** to death

119. **ignomy:** ignominy, disgrace

122. **close enacts:** secret purposes

123. **leer:** complexion

124. **slave:** rascal

125. **who should:** i.e., one who would

With all his threat'ning band of Typhon's brood,
Nor great Alcides, nor the god of war
Shall seize this prey out of his father's hands.   100
What, what, you sanguine, shallow-hearted boys,
You white-limed walls, you alehouse painted signs!
Coal black is better than another hue
In that it scorns to bear another hue;
For all the water in the ocean   105
Can never turn the swan's black legs to white,
Although she lave them hourly in the flood.
Tell the Empress from me, I am of age
To keep mine own, excuse it how she can.

DEMETRIUS
Wilt thou betray thy noble mistress thus?   110

AARON
My mistress is my mistress, this myself,
The vigor and the picture of my youth.
This before all the world do I prefer;
This maugre all the world will I keep safe,
Or some of you shall smoke for it in Rome.   115

DEMETRIUS
By this our mother is forever shamed.

CHIRON
Rome will despise her for this foul escape.

NURSE
The Emperor in his rage will doom her death.

CHIRON
I blush to think upon this ignomy.

AARON
Why, there's the privilege your beauty bears.   120
Fie, treacherous hue, that will betray with blushing
The close enacts and counsels of thy heart.
Here's a young lad framed of another leer.
Look how the black slave smiles upon the father,
As who should say "Old lad, I am thine own."   125

126. **sensibly:** perhaps, his senses, his body; or, perhaps, clearly

126–27. **fed / Of:** nourished with

127. **self:** same

130. **surer:** i.e., mother's (Proverbial: "The woman's side is the **surer** side.")

133. **Advise thee:** i.e., consider

134. **subscribe to:** i.e., assent to, agree with

135. **so we may:** provided that **we may**

137. **have the wind of you:** keep you under observation (as a hunter does downwind of prey)

141. **brave:** defy

142. **chafèd:** angered

149. **Two . . . away:** proverbial **keep counsel: keep** a secret

151. **to:** i.e., for

152. **Wherefore:** why

Tarquin's rape of Lucrece. (3.1.304; 4.1.64–65, 90–92)
From [Jost Amman,] *Icones Liuianae . . .* (1572).

He is your brother, lords, sensibly fed
Of that self blood that first gave life to you,
And from ⌜that⌝ womb where you imprisoned were
He is enfranchisèd and come to light.
Nay, he is your brother by the surer side,   130
Although my seal be stampèd in his face.

NURSE
Aaron, what shall I say unto the Empress?

DEMETRIUS
Advise thee, Aaron, what is to be done,
And we will all subscribe to thy advice.
Save thou the child, so we may all be safe.   135

AARON
Then sit we down, and let us all consult.
My son and I will have the wind of you.
Keep there. Now talk at pleasure of your safety.

DEMETRIUS, ⌜*to the Nurse*⌝
How many women saw this child of his?

AARON
Why, so, brave lords! When we join in league,   140
I am a lamb; but if you brave the Moor,
The chafèd boar, the mountain lioness,
The ocean swells not so as Aaron storms.
⌜*To the Nurse.*⌝ But say again, how many saw the
    child?   145

NURSE
Cornelia the midwife and myself,
And no one else but the delivered Empress.

AARON
The Empress, the midwife, and yourself.
Two may keep counsel when the third's away.
Go to the Empress; tell her this I said.   150
                                        He kills her.
"Wheak, wheak"! So cries a pig preparèd to the spit.

DEMETRIUS
What mean'st thou, Aaron? Wherefore didst thou this?

153. **policy:** craftiness, cunning
157–58. **Muliteus . . . wife:** i.e., **Muliteus my** countryman's **wife**
160. **pack:** conspire, scheme
161. **the circumstance of all:** i.e., **all** the details
162. **by this:** i.e., through, or by means of, **this**
167. **physic:** medicine
168. **bestow:** i.e., provide (literally, pay for)
169. **grooms:** fellows
171. **presently:** immediately
172. **made away:** killed
177. **highly bound:** greatly obliged
181. **slave:** fellow, rascal

AARON
  O Lord, sir, 'tis a deed of policy.
  Shall she live to betray this guilt of ours,
  A long-tongued babbling gossip? No, lords, no.   155
  And now be it known to you my full intent:
  Not far one Muliteus my countryman
  His wife but yesternight was brought to bed.
  His child is like to her, fair as you are.
  Go pack with him, and give the mother gold,   160
  And tell them both the circumstance of all,
  And how by this their child shall be advanced
  And be receivèd for the Emperor's heir,
  And substituted in the place of mine,
  To calm this tempest whirling in the court;   165
  And let the Emperor dandle him for his own.
  Hark you, lords, you see I have given her physic,
                  ⌈*indicating the Nurse*⌉
  And you must needs bestow her funeral.
  The fields are near, and you are gallant grooms.
  This done, see that you take no longer days,   170
  But send the midwife presently to me.
  The midwife and the nurse well made away,
  Then let the ladies tattle what they please.
CHIRON
  Aaron, I see thou wilt not trust the air
  With secrets.   175
DEMETRIUS   For this care of Tamora,
  Herself and hers are highly bound to thee.
               ⌈*Demetrius and Chiron*⌉ *exit,*
                   ⌈*carrying the Nurse's body.*⌉
AARON
  Now to the Goths, as swift as swallow flies,
  There to dispose this treasure in mine arms
  And secretly to greet the Empress' friends.—   180
  Come on, you thick-lipped slave, I'll bear you hence,

182. **puts us to our shifts:** brings us to this extremity

185. **cabin:** lodge, dwell

4.3 Titus has his friends and family shoot arrows to which are attached messages to the gods begging that Justice (as the goddess Astraea) be returned to earth. When a country fellow enters on his way to the court, Titus gives him a letter to take to Saturninus.

----

2. **Sir:** a mock title

3. **Look:** make sure that, see that; **draw home:** i.e., **draw** back the bowstring so that the bow is fully bent; **straight:** immediately

4. **Terras Astraea reliquit: Astraea** [the goddess of justice] has left the earth (Latin; Ovid, *Metamorphoses* 1.150). Her departure initiates the Iron Age of violence and discord. (See picture, page 156.)

5. **Be you remembered:** remember

6. **take you to:** i.e., apply yourselves to

8. **Happily:** haply, perhaps

9. **there's:** i.e., there (**in the sea**) is

11. **mattock:** a farm tool like a pick

13. **Pluto's region:** the classical underworld, ruled by the god Pluto (See picture, page 152.)

19. **What time:** when; **suffrages:** votes

For it is you that puts us to our shifts.
I'll make you feed on berries and on roots,
And feed on curds and whey, and suck the goat,
And cabin in a cave, and bring you up   185
To be a warrior and command a camp.
                              He exits ⌐*with the baby.*⌐

                    ⌐Scene 3⌐

Enter Titus, old Marcus, ⌐*his son Publius,*⌐ *young*
Lucius, and other gentlemen (⌐*Caius and Sempronius*⌐*)*
with bows, and Titus bears the arrows with letters on
                  the ends of them.

TITUS
Come, Marcus, come. Kinsmen, this is the way.—
Sir boy, let me see your archery.
Look you draw home enough and 'tis there straight.—
Terras Astraea reliquit.
Be you remembered, Marcus, she's gone, she's fled.—   5
Sirs, take you to your tools. You, cousins, shall
Go sound the ocean and cast your nets;
Happily you may catch her in the sea;
Yet there's as little justice as at land.
No; Publius and Sempronius, you must do it.   10
'Tis you must dig with mattock and with spade,
And pierce the inmost center of the earth.
Then, when you come to Pluto's region,
I pray you, deliver him this petition.
Tell him it is for justice and for aid,   15
And that it comes from old Andronicus,
Shaken with sorrows in ungrateful Rome.
Ah, Rome! Well, well, I made thee miserable
What time I threw the people's suffrages
On him that thus doth tyrannize o'er me.   20

23. **her:** i.e., **Astraea**

24. **go pipe for:** i.e., **go** whistle **for;** seek in vain **for**

25. **heavy:** sorrowful

26. **distract:** driven mad

28. **attend:** watch over

29. **feed:** i.e., indulge, cater to; **humor:** mood

30. **careful remedy: remedy** that shows care and concern

32. **But:** See longer note, page 212.

34. **wreak:** revenge

36. **how now:** an interjection meaning, loosely, **"how** is it **now"**

37. **What:** an interjection introducing a question; **her:** i.e., **Astraea**

39. **from:** i.e., come **from**

42. **perforce ... needs:** i.e., **you** are forced by circumstances to; **stay a time:** wait a while

44. **burning lake below:** perhaps, Phlegethon, a fiery river in the classical underworld

45. **Acheron:** i.e., hell (literally, a river in the classical underworld)

46. **shrubs ... cedars:** Proverbial: "High **cedars** fall when low **shrubs** remain."

47. **framed:** shaped, formed; **of ... size:** i.e., like a giant (The Cyclopes were mythical one-eyed giants; the most famous, Polyphemus, appears in book 9 of Homer's *Odyssey* and in Virgil's *Aeneid*.) See picture, page 160.

Go, get you gone, and pray be careful all,
And leave you not a man-of-war unsearched.
This wicked emperor may have shipped her hence,
And, kinsmen, then we may go pipe for justice.

MARCUS
O Publius, is not this a heavy case   25
To see thy noble uncle thus distract?

PUBLIUS
Therefore, my lords, it highly us concerns
By day and night t' attend him carefully,
And feed his humor kindly as we may,
Till time beget some careful remedy.   30

MARCUS
Kinsmen, his sorrows are past remedy
⌜But . . . . ⌝
Join with the Goths, and with revengeful war
Take wreak on Rome for this ingratitude,
And vengeance on the traitor Saturnine.   35

TITUS
Publius, how now? How now, my masters?
What, have you met with her?

PUBLIUS
No, my good lord, but Pluto sends you word,
If you will have Revenge from hell, you shall.
Marry, for Justice, she is so employed,   40
He thinks, with Jove in heaven, or somewhere else,
So that perforce you must needs stay a time.

TITUS
He doth me wrong to feed me with delays.
I'll dive into the burning lake below
And pull her out of Acheron by the heels.   45
Marcus, we are but shrubs, no cedars we,
No big-boned men framed of the Cyclops' size,
But metal, Marcus, steel to the very back,
Yet wrung with wrongs more than our backs can
    bear;   50

51. **sith:** since

53. **wreak:** avenge

54. **gear:** business

55–56. **Ad Jovem, Ad Apollinem, Ad Martem:** to Jove, to Apollo, to Mars (Latin) For these gods, see notes to 4.1.67 and 4.2.99.

57. **Pallas, Mercury:** See note to 4.1.67.

58. **Saturn:** the father of Jove (See picture, page 74.)

59. **were as good to:** i.e., might as well

60. **loose:** let fly, shoot

61. **Of my word:** i.e., upon **my word**

67. **in Virgo's lap:** i.e., into the constellation Virgo (often equated with Astraea) (See picture, page 156.)

71. **Taurus' horns:** Taurus is the constellation the **Bull** (line 73) (See picture below.)

73. **galled:** annoyed; or, perhaps, injured; **Aries:** the constellation the Ram

74–77. **That down ... present:** i.e., Aaron **the Moor** has given Saturninus a pair of **horns,** the customary headware of the cuckold   **villain:** servant

Taurus. (4.3.71, 73)
From Johann Engel, *Astrolabium* (1488).

And sith there's no justice in earth nor hell,
We will solicit heaven and move the gods
To send down Justice for to wreak our wrongs.
Come, to this gear. You are a good archer, Marcus.
He gives them the arrows.
"*Ad Jovem*," that's for you;—here, "*Ad Apollinem*";—   55
"*Ad Martem*," that's for myself;—
Here, boy, "to Pallas";—here, "to Mercury";—
"To ⌈Saturn,⌉" Caius—not to Saturnine!
You were as good to shoot against the wind.
To it, boy!—Marcus, loose when I bid.   60
Of my word, I have written to effect;
There's not a god left unsolicited.

MARCUS
Kinsmen, shoot all your shafts into the court.
We will afflict the Emperor in his pride.

TITUS
Now, masters, draw. (⌈*They shoot.*⌉) O, well said,   65
    Lucius!
Good boy, in Virgo's lap! Give it Pallas.

MARCUS
My lord, I aim a mile beyond the moon.
Your letter is with Jupiter by this.

TITUS
Ha, ha! Publius, Publius, what hast thou done?   70
See, see, thou hast shot off one of Taurus' horns!

MARCUS
This was the sport, my lord; when Publius shot,
The Bull, being galled, gave Aries such a knock
That down fell both the Ram's horns in the court,
And who should find them but the Empress' villain?   75
She laughed and told the Moor he should not choose
But give them to his master for a present.

TITUS
Why, there it goes. God give his Lordship joy!

78 SD. **country fellow:** The Quarto's name for this character, "Clown," could refer to the company's low-comic actor or to a rustic or peasant; hence our editorial substitution "country fellow," the role this character plays in the action.

79. **post:** special messenger

81. **Sirrah:** term of address to a male social inferior

84. **them:** the gibbet, or gallows

89. **carrier:** bearer of a message or letter

93. **press:** push myself forward

95. **tribunal plebs:** confusion for *tribuni plebis* (Latin, "tribunes of the people"), who function as judges; **take up:** settle amicably

96–97. **Emperal's:** confusion for "emperor's"

99. **oration:** petition

101–4. **Tell . . . life:** These lines are omitted by some modern editors on the grounds that they appear revised in lines 109–11.

102. **with a grace:** becomingly, gracefully

108. **Hold:** i.e., wait a minute

Enter ⌜*a country fellow*⌝ *with a basket and two
pigeons in it.*

News, news from heaven! Marcus, the post is
  come.—   80
  Sirrah, what tidings? Have you any letters?
  Shall I have Justice? What says Jupiter?
⌜COUNTRY FELLOW⌝ Ho, the gibbet-maker? He says that
  he hath taken them down again, for the man must
  not be hanged till the next week.   85
TITUS But what says Jupiter, I ask thee?
⌜COUNTRY FELLOW⌝ Alas, sir, I know not Jupiter; I never
  drank with him in all my life.
TITUS Why, villain, art not thou the carrier?
⌜COUNTRY FELLOW⌝ Ay, of my pigeons, sir; nothing else.   90
TITUS Why, didst thou not come from heaven?
⌜COUNTRY FELLOW⌝ From heaven? Alas, sir, I never
  came there. God forbid I should be so bold to press
  to heaven in my young days. Why, I am going with
  my pigeons to the tribunal plebs, to take up a mat-   95
  ter of brawl betwixt my uncle and one of the Emperal's men.
MARCUS, ⌜*to Titus*⌝ Why, sir, that is as fit as can be to
  serve for your oration; and let him deliver the pigeons to the Emperor from you.   100
TITUS Tell me, can you deliver an oration to the Emperor with a grace?
⌜COUNTRY FELLOW⌝ Nay, truly, sir, I could never say
  grace in all my life.
TITUS

Sirrah, come hither. Make no more ado,   105
But give your pigeons to the Emperor.
By me thou shalt have justice at his hands.
  Hold, hold; meanwhile here's money for thy

109. **charges:** troubles; or, perhaps, expenses
116. **bravely:** splendidly, handsomely
117. **warrant:** assure; **Let me alone:** i.e., leave it to me
120. **it:** possibly, **the oration;** possibly, the **knife** (The meaning of line 120 is obscure.)

4.4 Saturninus, enraged at the messages on the arrows, reads the letter brought by the country fellow and sentences him to death. Word comes that Lucius is leading the Goths against Rome. A message is sent to Lucius that Saturninus wishes to meet with him at Titus's house; meanwhile, Tamora sets out to charm Titus into helping them persuade Lucius to stop the attack.

———————

2. **overborne:** oppressed
3. **extent:** exercising

PLVTONIS IMAGO.

Pluto. (4.3.13)
From Georg Pictorius, *Apotheseos tam exterarum gentium quam Romanorum deorum* . . . (1558).

charges.—Give me pen and ink.—Sirrah, can you
with a grace deliver up a supplication?   110
⌜*He writes.*⌝

⌜COUNTRY FELLOW⌝   Ay, sir.

TITUS   Then here is a supplication for you, and when
you come to him, at the first approach you must
kneel, then kiss his foot, then deliver up your pigeons, and then look for your reward. I'll be at   115
hand, sir. See you do it bravely.
⌜*He hands him a paper.*⌝

⌜COUNTRY FELLOW⌝   I warrant you, sir. Let me alone.

TITUS
Sirrah, hast thou a knife? Come, let me see it.—
⌜*He takes the knife and gives it to Marcus.*⌝
Here, Marcus, fold it in the oration,
For thou hast made it like an humble suppliant.—   120
And when thou hast given it to the Emperor,
Knock at my door and tell me what he says.

⌜COUNTRY FELLOW⌝   God be with you, sir. I will.
He exits.

TITUS   Come, Marcus, let us go.—Publius, follow me.
They exit.

⌜Scene 4⌝

*Enter Emperor ⌜Saturninus⌝ and Empress ⌜Tamora⌝
and her two sons ⌜Chiron and Demetrius, with
Attendants.⌝ The Emperor brings the arrows in his
hand that Titus shot at him.*

SATURNINUS
Why, lords, what wrongs are these! Was ever seen
An emperor in Rome thus overborne,
Troubled, confronted thus, and for the extent
Of equal justice, used in such contempt?

5. **mightful:** mighty
7. **naught:** nothing
8. **even:** in exact agreement
9. **an if:** i.e., **if**
11. **wreaks:** acts of revenge
18. **blazoning:** proclaiming; **unjustice:** injustice
19. **goodly:** proper; admirable; **humor:** whim
24. **whom:** probably, Saturninus (If **whom** were to refer to **justice,** associated in this play with the goddess Astraea, then we would expect in lines 24 and 25 to be "she." Lines 24 and 25 are much debated and often emended.)
34. **meanest or the best:** i.e., lowest or the highest in rank (of the Andronici)
37. **High-witted:** clever; **gloze:** talk smoothly and speciously
38. **touched thee to the quick:** i.e., wounded you irreparably (*To the quick,* as used here, implies acute mental anguish.)
39. **Thy lifeblood:** i.e., once your **lifeblood** is

My lords, you know, ⌈as know⌉ the mightful gods,   5
However these disturbers of our peace
Buzz in the people's ears, there naught hath passed
But even with law against the willful sons
Of old Andronicus. And what an if
His sorrows have so overwhelmed his wits?   10
Shall we be thus afflicted in his wreaks,
His fits, his frenzy, and his bitterness?
And now he writes to heaven for his redress!
See, here's "to Jove," and this "to Mercury,"
This "to Apollo," this to the god of war.   15
Sweet scrolls to fly about the streets of Rome!
What's this but libeling against the Senate
And blazoning our unjustice everywhere?
A goodly humor is it not, my lords?
As who would say, in Rome no justice were.   20
But if I live, his feignèd ecstasies
Shall be no shelter to these outrages,
But he and his shall know that justice lives
In Saturninus' health, whom, if he sleep,
He'll so awake as he in fury shall   25
Cut off the proud'st conspirator that lives.

TAMORA
My gracious lord, my lovely Saturnine,
Lord of my life, commander of my thoughts,
Calm thee, and bear the faults of Titus' age,
Th' effects of sorrow for his valiant sons,   30
Whose loss hath pierced him deep and scarred his
    heart,
And rather comfort his distressèd plight
Than prosecute the meanest or the best
For these contempts. (⌈*Aside.*⌉) Why, thus it shall   35
    become
High-witted Tamora to gloze with all.
But, Titus, I have touched thee to the quick.
Thy lifeblood out, if Aaron now be wise,
Then is all safe, the anchor in the port.   40

43. **emperial:** perhaps confusion for "empress"

46. **good e'en:** good evening

48. **presently:** immediately

49. **must:** i.e., shall

51. **By'r Lady:** i.e., by Our Lady (an anachronistic oath on the Virgin Mary)

55. **device:** plot

60. **Nor:** neither; **shape privilege:** create immunity

62. **holp'st:** helped

63 SD. **nuntius:** messenger (Latin)

66. **gathered head:** raised a force; **power:** army

Astraea, goddess of justice, transformed into the
constellation Virgo. (4.3.4, 67)

From Hyginus, . . . *Fabularum liber* . . . (1535).

Enter ⌐Country Fellow.⌐

How now, good fellow, wouldst thou speak with us?
⌐COUNTRY FELLOW⌐   Yea, forsooth, an your Mistressship be
emperial.

TAMORA
Empress I am, but yonder sits the Emperor.
⌐COUNTRY FELLOW⌐   'Tis he!—God and Saint Stephen   45
give you good e'en. I have brought you a letter and
a couple of pigeons here.
                              ⌐Saturninus⌐ reads the letter.

SATURNINUS
Go, take him away, and hang him presently.
⌐COUNTRY FELLOW⌐   How much money must I have?
TAMORA   Come, sirrah, you must be hanged.   50
⌐COUNTRY FELLOW⌐   Hanged! ⌐By'r⌐ Lady, then I have
brought up a neck to a fair end.
                              He exits ⌐with Attendants.⌐

SATURNINUS
Despiteful and intolerable wrongs!
Shall I endure this monstrous villainy?
I know from whence this same device proceeds.   55
May this be borne?—as if his traitorous sons,
That died by law for murder of our brother,
Have by my means been butchered wrongfully!
Go, drag the villain hither by the hair.
Nor age nor honor shall shape privilege.   60
For this proud mock, I'll be thy slaughterman,
Sly, frantic wretch, that holp'st to make me great
In hope thyself should govern Rome and me.

Enter nuntius, Aemilius.

SATURNINUS   What news with thee, Aemilius?
AEMILIUS
Arm, my lords! Rome never had more cause.   65
The Goths have gathered head, and with a power

67. **bent . . . spoil:** ready to plunder
68. **amain:** at full speed; **conduct:** the command
71. **Coriolanus:** Banished from Rome, **Coriolanus** led an army of Volscians against the city. (See Shakespeare's play *Coriolanus,* and picture below.)
75. **begins:** i.e., begin
79. **wrongfully:** i.e., wrongful; or, **wrongfully** done
83. **succor:** help
85. **sun:** sunlight; **that:** i.e., because
86. **suffers:** allows
87. **careful:** i.e., full of anxiety concerning
89. **stint:** stop
90. **giddy:** foolish
94. **honey-stalks:** clover (which, when eaten in excess, causes liver rot in **sheep**)
95. **Whenas:** when

Coriolanus. (4.4.71)
From [Guillaume Rouillé,] . . . *Promptuarii iconum* . . . (1553).

Of high-resolvèd men bent to the spoil,
They hither march amain under conduct
Of Lucius, son to old Andronicus,
Who threats, in course of this revenge, to do   70
As much as ever Coriolanus did.

SATURNINUS
Is warlike Lucius general of the Goths?
These tidings nip me, and I hang the head
As flowers with frost or grass beat down with storms.
Ay, now begins our sorrows to approach.   75
'Tis he the common people love so much.
Myself hath often heard them say,
When I have walkèd like a private man,
That Lucius' banishment was wrongfully,
And they have wished that Lucius were their emperor.   80

TAMORA
Why should you fear? Is not your city strong?

SATURNINUS
Ay, but the citizens favor Lucius
And will revolt from me to succor him.

TAMORA
King, be thy thoughts imperious like thy name.
Is the sun dimmed that gnats do fly in it?   85
The eagle suffers little birds to sing
And is not careful what they mean thereby,
Knowing that with the shadow of his wings
He can at pleasure stint their melody.
Even so mayst thou the giddy men of Rome.   90
Then cheer thy spirit, for know, thou emperor,
I will enchant the old Andronicus
With words more sweet and yet more dangerous
Than baits to fish or honey-stalks to sheep,
Whenas the one is wounded with the bait,   95
The other rotted with delicious ⌐feed.⌐

SATURNINUS
But he will not entreat his son for us.

99. **smooth:** flatter

103. **before:** in advance; **ambassador:** official messenger

108. **stand in hostage:** insist on hostages

109. **pledge:** security

110. **do effectually:** i.e., accomplish (**Effectually** means "so as to answer the purpose.")

112. **temper:** persuade

115. **devices:** plots

116. **successantly:** an obscure word often emended by editors to "incessantly," meaning, perhaps, "immediately"

A Cyclops. (4.3.47)
From Ovid, . . . *Metamorphosin* . . . (1509).

160

TAMORA
   If Tamora entreat him, then he will,
   For I can smooth and fill his agèd ears
   With golden promises, that were his heart   100
   Almost impregnable, his old ⌜ears⌝ deaf,
   Yet should both ear and heart obey my tongue.
   ⌜*To Aemilius.*⌝ Go thou before to be our ambassador.
   Say that the Emperor requests a parley
   Of warlike Lucius, and appoint the meeting   105
   Even at his father's house, the old Andronicus.

SATURNINUS
   Aemilius, do this message honorably,
   And if he stand in hostage for his safety,
   Bid him demand what pledge will please him best.

AEMILIUS
   Your bidding shall I do effectually.   110
                              He exits.

TAMORA
   Now will I to that old Andronicus
   And temper him with all the art I have
   To pluck proud Lucius from the warlike Goths.
   And now, sweet emperor, be blithe again,
   And bury all thy fear in my devices.   115

SATURNINUS
   Then go successantly, and plead to him.
                              They exit.

TITUS
ANDRONICUS

ACT 5

5.1 Aaron is captured by Lucius and his army of Goths. After Lucius swears to protect the baby, Aaron confesses to the series of horrors he has committed. When the messenger from Saturninus arrives, Lucius agrees to come to Rome to meet with the Emperor.

- - - - - - - -

1. **Approvèd:** proven, tested
2. **letters:** i.e., a letter (*litterae*, Latin)
7. **scathe:** harm
8. **him:** i.e., Saturninus
9. **slip:** scion, descendant
12. **Ingrateful:** ungrateful
13. **bold:** confident
15. **master: Bees** were believed to have a king, not a queen.
19. **lusty:** vigorous

Hercules. (4.2.99)
From Vincenzo Cartari, *Le vere e noue imagini* . . . (1615).

⟨ACT 5⟩

⌜Scene 1⌝

⟨Flourish.⟩ Enter Lucius with an army of Goths, with
Drums and Soldiers.

LUCIUS
  Approvèd warriors and my faithful friends,
  I have receivèd letters from great Rome
  Which signifies what hate they bear their emperor
  And how desirous of our sight they are.
  Therefore, great lords, be as your titles witness,   5
  Imperious, and impatient of your wrongs,
  And wherein Rome hath done you any scathe,
  Let him make treble satisfaction.
⌜FIRST⌝ GOTH
  Brave slip sprung from the great Andronicus,
  Whose name was once our terror, now our comfort,   10
  Whose high exploits and honorable deeds
  Ingrateful Rome rèquites with foul contempt,
  Be bold in us. We'll follow where thou lead'st,
  Like stinging bees in hottest summer's day
  Led by their master to the flowered fields,   15
  And be avenged on cursèd Tamora.
⌜GOTHS⌝
  And as he saith, so say we all with him.
LUCIUS
  I humbly thank him, and I thank you all.
  But who comes here, led by a lusty Goth?

21. **monastery:** an anachronistic reference to a Roman Catholic house for monks

22. **earnestly:** intensely

24. **underneath:** below

25. **made unto:** went toward

26. **controlled:** reproved

27. **tawny:** brown or black; **slave:** Like **brat** and **villain,** this word need not be abusive in this context.

27. **dame:** mother

28. **bewray:** reveal, make known

33. **rates:** chides, scolds

36. **hold:** regard, esteem

38. **Surprised:** captured

39. **To use . . . of the man:** i.e., for **you** to deal with **the man as you think** necessary

42. **This . . . eye:** Proverbial: "A black man is a **pearl** in a fair woman's **eye.**"

44. **wall-eyed:** perhaps, glaring

Enter a Goth, leading of Aaron with his child in his arms.

⌈SECOND⌉ GOTH
  Renownèd Lucius, from our troops I strayed   20
  To gaze upon a ruinous monastery,
  And as I earnestly did fix mine eye
  Upon the wasted building, suddenly
  I heard a child cry underneath a wall.
  I made unto the noise, when soon I heard   25
  The crying babe controlled with this discourse:
  "Peace, tawny slave, half me and half thy dame!
  Did not thy hue bewray whose brat thou art,
  Had nature lent thee but thy mother's look,
  Villain, thou mightst have been an emperor.   30
  But where the bull and cow are both milk white,
  They never do beget a coal-black calf.
  Peace, villain, peace!"—even thus he rates the babe—
  "For I must bear thee to a trusty Goth
  Who, when he knows thou art the Empress' babe,   35
  Will hold thee dearly for thy mother's sake."
  With this, my weapon drawn, I rushed upon him,
  Surprised him suddenly, and brought him hither
  To use as you think needful of the man.

LUCIUS
  O worthy Goth, this is the incarnate devil   40
  That robbed Andronicus of his good hand;
  This is the pearl that pleased your empress' eye;
  And here's the base fruit of her burning lust.—
  Say, wall-eyed slave, whither wouldst thou convey
  This growing image of thy fiendlike face?   45
  Why dost not speak? What, deaf? Not a word?—
  A halter, soldiers! Hang him on this tree,
  And by his side his fruit of bastardy.

AARON
  Touch not the boy. He is of royal blood.

50. **for ever being good:** i.e., **ever** to be **good**

51. **sprawl:** convulse at the moment of death

52. **withal:** with

56. **show thee:** make known to you, expound (The phrase **"show thee wondrous things"** carries a sardonic religious resonance, since in the Bible it is used to describe God's and Moses' working of miracles. See Nehemiah 9.10 and Acts 7.36.)

61. **nourished:** nursed; brought up

66. **Complots:** plots

67. **Ruthful:** lamentable; **piteously performed: performed** in a manner that excites pity

70. **Tell on:** i.e., speak

75. **for:** because

77. **popish:** an anachronistic Protestant term of contempt meaning "Roman Catholic"

LUCIUS
Too like the sire for ever being good. 50
First hang the child, that he may see it sprawl,
A sight to vex the father's soul withal.
Get me a ladder.
⌜*A ladder is brought, which Aaron is made to climb.*⌝
AARON   Lucius, save the child
And bear it from me to the Empress. 55
If thou do this, I'll show thee wondrous things
That highly may advantage thee to hear.
If thou wilt not, befall what may befall,
I'll speak no more but "Vengeance rot you all!"

LUCIUS
Say on, and if it please me which thou speak'st, 60
Thy child shall live, and I will see it nourished.

AARON
And if it please thee? Why, assure thee, Lucius,
'Twill vex thy soul to hear what I shall speak;
For I must talk of murders, rapes, and massacres,
Acts of black night, abominable deeds, 65
Complots of mischief, treason, villainies,
Ruthful to hear, yet piteously performed.
And this shall all be buried in my death,
Unless thou swear to me my child shall live.

LUCIUS
Tell on thy mind. I say thy child shall live. 70

AARON
Swear that he shall, and then I will begin.

LUCIUS
Who should I swear by? Thou believest no god.
That granted, how canst thou believe an oath?

AARON
What if I do not? As indeed I do not.
Yet, for I know thou art religious 75
And hast a thing within thee callèd conscience,
With twenty popish tricks and ceremonies

79. **urge:** demand; **for that:** because
80. **holds . . . god:** regards his fool's mock scepter as **a god** (See picture below.)
86. **discover:** reveal
89. **luxurious:** lecherous
91. **To:** compared **to; anon:** soon
98. **Trim:** excellent
101. **codding:** perhaps, lecherous (The word is not recorded as occurring elsewhere. *Cod* is an impolite word for the scrotum.)
102. **As sure . . . set:** proverbial   **set:** game (of cards)
104. **fought at head:** i.e., attacked head on
105. **witness of:** i.e., **witness** to

A Fool with his bauble. (5.1.80)
From Stephen Batman, *The trauayled pylgrime . . .* (1569).

Which I have seen thee careful to observe,
Therefore I urge thy oath; for that I know
An idiot holds his bauble for a god   80
And keeps the oath which by that god he swears,
To that I'll urge him. Therefore thou shalt vow
By that same god, what god soe'er it be
That thou adorest and hast in reverence,
To save my boy, to nourish and bring him up,   85
Or else I will discover naught to thee.

LUCIUS
Even by my god I swear to thee I will.

AARON
First know thou, I begot him on the Empress.

LUCIUS
O, most insatiate and luxurious woman!

AARON
Tut, Lucius, this was but a deed of charity   90
To that which thou shalt hear of me anon.
'Twas her two sons that murdered Bassianus.
They cut thy sister's tongue, and ravished her,
And cut her hands, and trimmed her as thou sawest.

LUCIUS
O detestable villain, call'st thou that trimming?   95

AARON
Why, she was washed, and cut, and trimmed; and
    'twas
Trim sport for them which had the doing of it.

LUCIUS
O, barbarous beastly villains, like thyself!

AARON
Indeed, I was their tutor to instruct them.   100
That codding spirit had they from their mother,
As sure a card as ever won the set;
That bloody mind I think they learned of me,
As true a dog as ever fought at head.
Well, let my deeds be witness of my worth.   105

106. **trained:** enticed; **guileful:** treacherous
110. **Confederate:** i.e., in league
111. **what not:** i.e., **what** was **not**
113. **cheater:** (1) cheat; (2) escheator, or officer appointed to look after property forfeited to the crown
115. **broke my heart:** i.e., died
116. **pried me:** peered, spied
117. **for his hand:** i.e., in exchange **for his hand**
121. **sounded almost:** i.e., **almost** swooned
124. **like a black dog:** "To blush **like a black dog**" is a proverb with ironic meaning.
129. **ill:** evil
131. **maid:** virgin
132. **forswear:** perjure
135. **haystalks:** haystacks
138. **friends':** relatives'

I trained thy brethren to that guileful hole
Where the dead corpse of Bassianus lay.
I wrote the letter that thy father found,
And hid the gold within that letter mentioned,
Confederate with the Queen and her two sons.   110
And what not done that thou hast cause to rue,
Wherein I had no stroke of mischief in it?
I played the cheater for thy father's hand,
And, when I had it, drew myself apart
And almost broke my heart with extreme laughter.   115
I pried me through the crevice of a wall
When, for his hand, he had his two sons' heads,
Beheld his tears, and laughed so heartily
That both mine eyes were rainy like to his.
And when I told the Empress of this sport,   120
She sounded almost at my pleasing tale,
And for my tidings gave me twenty kisses.

GOTH
What, canst thou say all this and never blush?

AARON
Ay, like a black dog, as the saying is.

LUCIUS
Art thou not sorry for these heinous deeds?   125

AARON
Ay, that I had not done a thousand more.
Even now I curse the day—and yet, I think,
Few come within the compass of my curse—
Wherein I did not some notorious ill,
As kill a man, or else devise his death;   130
Ravish a maid or plot the way to do it;
Accuse some innocent and forswear myself;
Set deadly enmity between two friends;
Make poor men's cattle break their necks;
Set fire on barns and haystalks in the night,   135
And bid the owners quench them with their tears.
Oft have I digged up dead men from their graves
And set them upright at their dear friends' door,

144. **As willingly:** with as ready a will
148. **presently:** immediately
155. **Desires:** i.e., who **desires**
160. **for he:** i.e., because he
162. **your hostages:** i.e., whomever you choose to hold as **hostages**
165. **pledges:** hostages

"Would I were a devil . . . in everlasting fire . . . so I might . . . torment you." (5.1.149–52)
From Johann Weichard von Valvasor,
Theatrum mortis humanae . . . (1682).

Even when their sorrows almost was forgot,
And on their skins, as on the bark of trees,   140
Have with my knife carvèd in Roman letters
"Let not your sorrow die, though I am dead."
But I have done a thousand dreadful things
As willingly as one would kill a fly,
And nothing grieves me heartily indeed   145
But that I cannot do ten thousand more.

LUCIUS
Bring down the devil, for he must not die
So sweet a death as hanging presently.
           ⌈*Aaron is brought down from the ladder.*⌉

AARON
If there be devils, would I were a devil,
To live and burn in everlasting fire,   150
So I might have your company in hell
But to torment you with my bitter tongue.

LUCIUS
Sirs, stop his mouth, and let him speak no more.

              Enter Aemilius.

GOTH
My lord, there is a messenger from Rome
Desires to be admitted to your presence.   155

LUCIUS   Let him come near. ⌈*Aemilius comes forward.*⌉
Welcome, Aemilius. What's the news from Rome?

AEMILIUS
Lord Lucius, and you princes of the Goths,
The Roman Emperor greets you all by me;
And, for he understands you are in arms,   160
He craves a parley at your father's house,
Willing you to demand your hostages,
And they shall be immediately delivered.

GOTH
What says our general?

LUCIUS
Aemilius, let the Emperor give his pledges   165

5.2   Tamora, disguised as Revenge, tells Titus she has come to his aid, and that if he will invite Lucius to a feast, she will bring Tamora and Saturninus so that Titus can avenge himself on them. When she leaves, Titus insists that her companions, "Rape" and "Murder" (Chiron and Demetrius in disguise), remain with him until her return. He then cuts their throats and collects the blood, which he will mix with their ground bones into pastry for a pie to be served to Tamora.

---

1. **sad habiliment:** sober-colored costume
2. **encounter with:** meet
5. **study:** i.e., door to his **study; keeps:** stays
8. **confusion:** destruction
11. **sad:** solemn; **fly away:** perhaps an allusion to the Sibyl's prophecies (See 4.1.106.)
18. **Wanting:** lacking; **give it action:** i.e., supplement **my talk** with appropriate gestures in the style of classical oratory
19. **odds of:** i.e., advantage over

Unto my father and my uncle Marcus,
And we will come. March away.

⌐*They exit.*⌐

⌐Scene 2⌐

Enter Tamora and her two sons, disguised.

TAMORA
 Thus, in this strange and sad habiliment
 I will encounter with Andronicus
 And say I am Revenge, sent from below
 To join with him and right his heinous wrongs.
 Knock at his study, where they say he keeps   5
 To ruminate strange plots of dire revenge.
 Tell him Revenge is come to join with him
 And work confusion on his enemies.

They knock, and Titus (⌐above⌐) opens his study door.

TITUS
 Who doth molest my contemplation?
 Is it your trick to make me ope the door,   10
 That so my sad decrees may fly away
 And all my study be to no effect?
 You are deceived, for what I mean to do,
 See here, in bloody lines I have set down,
 And what is written shall be executed.   15
TAMORA
 Titus, I am come to talk with thee.
TITUS
 No, not a word. How can I grace my talk,
 Wanting a hand to give ⟨it action?⟩
 Thou hast the odds of me; therefore, no more.
TAMORA
 If thou didst know me, thou wouldst talk with me.   20

32. **gnawing vulture:** perhaps an allusion to the Prometheus story (See note to 2.1.17 and picture, page 82.)

33. **wreakful:** vengeful (an apparently deliberate redundancy of expression)

37. **obscurity:** dark place

39. **couch:** hide

46. **Rape and Murder:** See longer note, page 212.

47. **surance:** assurance, guarantee

48. **tear . . . wheels:** Large **wheels** were used as instruments of torture. Criminals were tied to such **wheels** and their bodies broken or "torn."

49. **wagoner:** charioteer

50. **about:** around

51. **proper:** handsome

52. **hale:** pull

An emblematic image of Revenge. (5.2.3)
From Cesare Ripa, *Iconologie* . . . (1677).

TITUS
  I am not mad. I know thee well enough.
  Witness this wretched stump; witness these crimson
    lines;
  Witness these trenches made by grief and care;
  Witness the tiring day and heavy night;   25
  Witness all sorrow that I know thee well
  For our proud empress, mighty Tamora.
  Is not thy coming for my other hand?

TAMORA
  Know, thou sad man, I am not Tamora.
  She is thy enemy, and I thy friend.   30
  I am Revenge, sent from th' infernal kingdom
  To ease the gnawing vulture of thy mind
  By working wreakful vengeance on thy foes.
  Come down and welcome me to this world's light.
  Confer with me of murder and of death.   35
  There's not a hollow cave or lurking-place,
  No vast obscurity or misty vale
  Where bloody murder or detested rape
  Can couch for fear but I will find them out,
  And in their ears tell them my dreadful name,   40
  Revenge, which makes the foul offender quake.

TITUS
  Art thou Revenge? And art thou sent to me
  To be a torment to mine enemies?

TAMORA
  I am. Therefore come down and welcome me.

TITUS
  Do me some service ere I come to thee.   45
  Lo, by thy side, where Rape and Murder stands,
  Now give some surance that thou art Revenge:
  Stab them, or tear them on thy chariot wheels,
  And then I'll come and be thy wagoner,
  And whirl along with thee about the ⌐globe,⌐   50
  Provide thee two proper palfreys, black as jet,
  To hale thy vengeful wagon swift away,

54. **car:** chariot

57. **Hyperion's:** i.e., the sun's (In Greek mythology Hyperion, one of the Titans, was the father of the sun.)

60. **So thou:** i.e., if you will; **Rapine:** i.e., rape

64. **vengeance of:** i.e., **vengeance** on

66. **worldly:** mortal, of this world

71. **closing:** agreeing

72. **forge:** invent; **humors:** whims

77. **sure:** securely

78. **practice:** scheme; **out of hand:** at once; extempore

79. **giddy:** flighty, foolish

The sun "in his glistering coach." (2.1.5–8)

From Claude François Menestrier, *L'art des emblemes* . . . (1684).

And find out ⌜murderers⌝ in their guilty ⌜caves.⌝
And when thy car is loaden with their heads,
I will dismount and by thy wagon wheel   55
Trot like a servile footman all day long,
Even from ⌜Hyperion's⌝ rising in the east
Until his very downfall in the sea.
And day by day I'll do this heavy task,
So thou destroy Rapine and Murder there.   60

TAMORA
These are my ministers and come with me.

TITUS
Are ⌜they⌝ thy ministers? What are they called?

TAMORA
Rape and Murder; therefore callèd so
'Cause they take vengeance of such kind of men.

TITUS
Good Lord, how like the Empress' sons they are,   65
And you the Empress! But we ⌜worldly⌝ men
Have miserable, mad, mistaking eyes.
O sweet Revenge, now do I come to thee,
And if one arm's embracement will content thee,
I will embrace thee in it by and by.   70
                              ⌜*He exits above.*⌝

TAMORA
This closing with him fits his lunacy.
Whate'er I forge to feed his brainsick humors,
Do you uphold and maintain in your speeches,
For now he firmly takes me for Revenge;
And, being credulous in this mad thought,   75
I'll make him send for Lucius his son;
And whilst I at a banquet hold him sure,
I'll find some cunning practice out of hand
To scatter and disperse the giddy Goths,
Or, at the least, make them his enemies.   80
See, here he comes, and I must ply my theme.

83. **Fury:** In mythology, a **Fury** (one of the Greek Erinyes) was a serpent-haired goddess who exacted punishment for crimes.

86. **Well are you fitted:** i.e., how much you would resemble them

88. **wot:** know; **wags:** stirs

91. **convenient:** appropriate, suitable

100. **that's like:** i.e., who resembles

103. **hap:** chance, luck

108. **attended:** waited upon, accompanied

109. **by thine own proportion:** i.e., by reference to your own shape or figure

A hart at bay. (4.2.43)
From [George Turberville,] *The noble art of venerie or hunting . . .* (1611).

⌜*Enter Titus.*⌝

TITUS
Long have I been forlorn, and all for thee.
Welcome, dread Fury, to my woeful house.—
Rapine and Murder, you are welcome too.
How like the Empress and her sons you are!   85
Well are you fitted, had you but a Moor.
Could not all hell afford you such a devil?
For well I wot the Empress never wags
But in her company there is a Moor;
And, would you represent our queen aright,   90
It were convenient you had such a devil.
But welcome as you are. What shall we do?

TAMORA
What wouldst thou have us do, Andronicus?

DEMETRIUS
Show me a murderer; I'll deal with him.

CHIRON
Show me a villain that hath done a rape,   95
And I am sent to be revenged on him.

TAMORA
Show me a thousand that hath done thee wrong,
And I will be revengèd on them all.

TITUS, ⌜*to Demetrius*⌝
Look round about the wicked streets of Rome,
And when thou findst a man that's like thyself,   100
Good Murder, stab him; he's a murderer.
⌜*To Chiron.*⌝ Go thou with him, and when it is thy
    hap
To find another that is like to thee,
Good Rapine, stab him; he is a ravisher.   105
⌜*To Tamora.*⌝ Go thou with them; and in the
    Emperor's court
There is a queen attended by a Moor.
Well shalt thou know her by thine own proportion,

110. **up and down:** head to toe; altogether
113. **lessoned:** instructed
118. **solemn:** sumptuous, ceremonious
127. **repair:** come

The. xv. Bookes
of P. Ouidius Naso, entytuled
Metamorphosis, translated oute of
Latin into English meeter, by Ar-
thur Golding Gentleman,
A worke very pleasaunt
and delectable.

With skill, heede, and iudgement, this worke must be read,
For else to the Reader it standes in small stead.

1 5   67

Imprynted at London, by
Willyam Seres.

Title page of Golding's translation of
Ovid's *Metamorphoses* (1567). (4.1.43)

For up and down she doth resemble thee.   110
I pray thee, do on them some violent death.
They have been violent to me and mine.

TAMORA
Well hast thou lessoned us; this shall we do.
But would it please thee, good Andronicus,
To send for Lucius, thy thrice-valiant son,   115
Who leads towards Rome a band of warlike Goths,
And bid him come and banquet at thy house?
When he is here, even at thy solemn feast,
I will bring in the Empress and her sons,
The Emperor himself, and all thy foes,   120
And at thy mercy shall they stoop and kneel,
And on them shalt thou ease thy angry heart.
What says Andronicus to this device?

TITUS, (⌜*calling*⌝)
Marcus, my brother, 'tis sad Titus calls.

Enter Marcus.

Go, gentle Marcus, to thy nephew Lucius.   125
Thou shalt inquire him out among the Goths.
Bid him repair to me and bring with him
Some of the chiefest princes of the Goths.
Bid him encamp his soldiers where they are.
Tell him the Emperor and the Empress too   130
Feast at my house, and he shall feast with them.
This do thou for my love, and so let him,
As he regards his agèd father's life.

MARCUS
This will I do, and soon return again. ⌜*Marcus exits.*⌝

TAMORA
Now will I hence about thy business   135
And take my ministers along with me.

TITUS
Nay, nay, let Rape and Murder stay with me,
Or else I'll call my brother back again
And cleave to no revenge but Lucius.

142. **governed our determined jest:** managed the **jest** that we had decided on

143. **smooth:** flatter; **speak him fair: speak** kindly to him

144. **turn again:** return

146. **o'erreach:** get the better of; **devices:** schemes, plots

147. **dam:** mother

148. **at pleasure:** i.e., when you wish

150. **complot:** plot

157. **take them:** i.e., **take them** to be

TAMORA, ⌜*aside to Chiron and Demetrius*⌝
 What say you, boys? Will you abide with him   140
 Whiles I go tell my lord the Emperor
 How I have governed our determined jest?
 Yield to his humor, smooth and speak him fair,
 And tarry with him till I turn again.

TITUS, ⌜*aside*⌝
 I knew them all, though they supposed me mad,   145
 And will o'erreach them in their own devices—
 A pair of cursèd hellhounds and their dam!

DEMETRIUS, ⌜*aside to Tamora*⌝
 Madam, depart at pleasure. Leave us here.

TAMORA
 Farewell, Andronicus. Revenge now goes
 To lay a complot to betray thy foes.   150

TITUS
 I know thou dost; and, sweet Revenge, farewell.
        ⌜*Tamora exits.*⌝

CHIRON
 Tell us, old man, how shall we be employed?

TITUS
 Tut, I have work enough for you to do.—
 Publius, come hither; Caius, and Valentine.

   ⌜*Publius, Caius, and Valentine enter.*⌝

PUBLIUS What is your will?   155
TITUS Know you these two?
PUBLIUS
 The Empress' sons, I take them—Chiron, Demetrius.

TITUS
 Fie, Publius, fie, thou art too much deceived.
 The one is Murder, and Rape is the other's name;
 And therefore bind them, gentle Publius.   160
 Caius and Valentine, lay hands on them.

163. **sure:** securely
164. **cry:** i.e., **cry** out
166. **therefore:** for that reason
167. **Stop:** cover, plug; **close:** tightly
168. **fast:** tightly
171. **fearful:** dreadful
181. **constrained:** violated
184. **martyr:** cruelly kill

To bake Chickens or Pigeons.

Take either six pigeon peepers or six chicken peepers, if big cut them in quarters, then take three sweet-breads 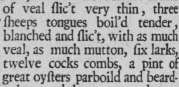 of veal slic't very thin, three sheeps tongues boil'd tender, blanched and slic't, with as much veal, as much mutton, six larks, twelve cocks combs, a pint of great oysters parboild and bearded, calves udder cut in pieces, and three marrow bones,

A pastry shell or "coffin." (5.2.192)
From Robert May, *The accomplisht cook* . . . (1685).

Oft have you heard me wish for such an hour,
And now I find it. Therefore bind them sure,
And stop their mouths if they begin to cry.
⌐*Titus exits.*⌐

CHIRON
Villains, forbear! We are the Empress' sons.   165

PUBLIUS
And therefore do we what we are commanded.—
Stop close their mouths; let them not speak a word.
Is he sure bound? Look that you bind them fast.

Enter Titus Andronicus with a knife, and Lavinia
with a basin.

TITUS
Come, come, Lavinia. Look, thy foes are bound.—
Sirs, stop their mouths. Let them not speak to me,   170
But let them hear what fearful words I utter.—
O villains, Chiron and Demetrius!
Here stands the spring whom you have stained with
    mud,
This goodly summer with your winter mixed.   175
You killed her husband, and for that vile fault
Two of her brothers were condemned to death,
My hand cut off and made a merry jest,
Both her sweet hands, her tongue, and that more dear
Than hands or tongue, her spotless chastity,   180
Inhuman traitors, you constrained and forced.
What would you say if I should let you speak?
Villains, for shame you could not beg for grace.
Hark, wretches, how I mean to martyr you.
This one hand yet is left to cut your throats,   185
Whiles that Lavinia 'tween her stumps doth hold
The basin that receives your guilty blood.
You know your mother means to feast with me,
And calls herself Revenge, and thinks me mad.
Hark, villains, I will grind your bones to dust,   190

192. **a coffin . . . rear:** i.e., **I will** raise a free-standing pie crust (See picture, page 188.)

193. **pasties:** pies

195. **Like . . . increase:** In Sonnet 19, Time makes "the earth devour her own sweet brood" (line 2). **increase:** offspring, children

197. **surfeit:** feast gluttonously

198. **Philomel:** See notes to 2.3.43, 2.4.38–39, and Appendix.

199. **Procne:** The wife of Tereus and sister of Philomela, **Procne** took vengeance for her sister's rape by killing her own son, cooking him, and feeding him to his unknowing father. (See Appendix, where Golding's spelling of her name is "Progne.") See picture, page 194.

203. **small:** fine

204. **with this . . . temper it:** i.e., moisten it with this blood

206. **officious:** zealously dutiful

208. **stern:** terrible, merciless; **Centaurs' feast:** an infamous wedding **feast** at which erupted a bloody battle between the Lapithae (whose king's marriage was being celebrated) and Centaurs (creatures half-man, half-horse) who were their guests (See Ovid's *Metamorphoses* 12.)

210. **against . . . comes:** in time for the arrival of **their mother**

5.3 At the feast, Titus serves the pie made from the bodies of Chiron and Demetrius. He then stabs Lavinia, reveals the actions and the fate of Tamora's sons, and stabs Tamora. Saturninus kills Titus and

(continued)

And with your blood and it I'll make a paste,
And of the paste a coffin I will rear,
And make two pasties of your shameful heads,
And bid that strumpet, your unhallowed dam,
Like to the earth swallow her own increase.   195
This is the feast that I have bid her to,
And this the banquet she shall surfeit on;
For worse than Philomel you used my daughter,
And worse than Procne I will be revenged.
And now prepare your throats.—Lavinia, come,   200
Receive the blood.   *He cuts their throats.*
                          And when that they are dead,
Let me go grind their bones to powder small,
And with this hateful liquor temper it,
And in that paste let their vile heads be baked.   205
Come, come, be everyone officious
To make this banquet, which I wish may prove
More stern and bloody than the Centaurs' feast.
So. Now bring them in, for I'll play the cook
And see them ready against their mother comes.   210
              They exit, ⌜*carrying the dead bodies.*⌝

                    ⌜Scene 3⌝

Enter Lucius, Marcus, and the Goths, ⌜*with Aaron,*
    Guards, and an Attendant carrying the baby.⌝

LUCIUS
    Uncle Marcus, since 'tis my father's mind
    That I repair to Rome, I am content.
⌜FIRST⌝ GOTH
    And ours with thine, befall what fortune will.
LUCIUS
    Good uncle, take you in this barbarous Moor,
    This ravenous tiger, this accursèd devil.   5
    Let him receive no sust'nance. Fetter him

Lucius kills Saturninus. Marcus and Lucius address the Romans, recounting the horrors perpetrated by Tamora and Aaron. Lucius is hailed as the new emperor. Aaron is condemned to a dreadful death, and Titus is mourned by Marcus, Lucius, and Young Lucius.

------

1. **mind:** desire, wish
2. **repair:** come
3. **ours:** perhaps, our minds; **befall . . . will:** i.e., whatever happens
4. **in:** i.e., into Titus's house (See line 124.)
18. **boots:** avails, profits
19. **break:** begin; **parle:** meeting to discuss terms under a truce
20. **quarrels:** complaints, charges
21. **careful:** sorrowful
23. **league:** alliance

Till he be brought unto the Empress' face
For testimony of her foul proceedings.
And see the ambush of our friends be strong.
I fear the Emperor means no good to us.   10

AARON
Some devil whisper curses in my ear
And prompt me that my tongue may utter forth
The venomous malice of my swelling heart.

LUCIUS
Away, inhuman dog, unhallowed slave!—
Sirs, help our uncle to convey him in.   15
                              Sound trumpets.
The trumpets show the Emperor is at hand.
                    ⌜*Guards and Aaron exit.*⌝

Enter Emperor ⌜*Saturninus*⌝ *and Empress* ⌜*Tamora*⌝
with ⌜*Aemilius,*⌝ *Tribunes,* ⌜*Attendants,*⌝ *and others.*

SATURNINUS
What, hath the firmament more suns than one?

LUCIUS
What boots it thee to call thyself a sun?

MARCUS
Rome's emperor, and nephew, break the parle.
These quarrels must be quietly debated.   20
The feast is ready which the careful Titus
Hath ordained to an honorable end,
For peace, for love, for league and good to Rome.
Please you therefore draw nigh and take your places.

SATURNINUS   Marcus, we will.   25

*Trumpets sounding, enter Titus like a cook, placing the
dishes,* ⌜*with young Lucius and others,*⌝ *and Lavinia
with a veil over her face.*

TITUS
Welcome, my lord;—welcome, dread queen;—
Welcome, you warlike Goths;—welcome, Lucius;—

28. **cheer:** hospitable entertainment, food
33. **beholding:** beholden, obliged
34. **An if:** i.e., **if**
35. **resolve:** answer
36–38. **Virginius . . . deflowered: Virginius** was a Roman centurion who killed his raped **daughter. enforced:** raped, overcome by violence
41. **Because:** so that, in order that
42. **still:** continually
43. **effectual:** valid
44. **lively:** vivid
48. **unkind:** unnatural; cruel; villainous

Procne's revenge. (5.2.199)
From Gabriele Simeoni, *La vita . . .* (1559).

And welcome, all. Although the cheer be poor,
'Twill fill your stomachs. Please you eat of it.
⌐*They begin to eat.*⌐

SATURNINUS
  Why art thou thus attired, Andronicus?   30

TITUS
  Because I would be sure to have all well
  To entertain your Highness and your empress.

TAMORA
  We are beholding to you, good Andronicus.

TITUS
  An if your Highness knew my heart, you were.—
  My lord the Emperor, resolve me this: 35
  Was it well done of rash Virginius
  To slay his daughter with his own right hand
  Because she was enforced, stained, and deflowered?

SATURNINUS   It was, Andronicus.

TITUS   Your reason, mighty lord?   40

SATURNINUS
  Because the girl should not survive her shame,
  And by her presence still renew his sorrows.

TITUS
  A reason mighty, strong, and effectual;
  A pattern, precedent, and lively warrant
  For me, most wretched, to perform the like.   45
  Die, die, Lavinia, and thy shame with thee,
  And with thy shame thy father's sorrow die.
⌐*He kills Lavinia.*⌐

SATURNINUS
  What hast thou done, unnatural and unkind?

TITUS
  Killed her for whom my tears have made me blind.
  I am as woeful as Virginius was,   50
  And have a thousand times more cause than he
  To do this outrage, and it now is done.

60. **presently:** immediately
62. **daintily:** i.e., with delicate attention to the taste
67. **meed:** recompense
69. **severed:** dispersed
72. **corn:** wheat, or stalks of wheat; **mutual:** common, collective (See picture below.)
74. **bane:** death, destruction
75. **she:** i.e., Rome

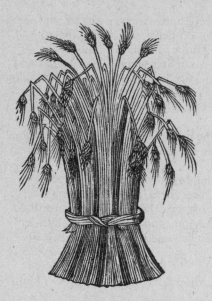

"Scattered corn" knit "into one mutual sheaf." (5.3.71–72)
From Geoffrey Whitney, *A choice of emblemes* . . . (1586).

SATURNINUS
  What, was she ravished? Tell who did the deed.

TITUS
  Will't please you eat?—Will't please your Highness
    feed?   55

TAMORA
  Why hast thou slain thine only daughter thus?

TITUS
  Not I; 'twas Chiron and Demetrius.
  They ravished her and cut away her tongue,
  And they, 'twas they, that did her all this wrong.

SATURNINUS
  Go fetch them hither to us presently.   60

TITUS
  Why, there they are, both bakèd in this pie,
  Whereof their mother daintily hath fed,
  Eating the flesh that she herself hath bred.
  'Tis true, 'tis true! Witness my knife's sharp point.
                              He stabs the Empress.

SATURNINUS
  Die, frantic wretch, for this accursèd deed.   65
                              ⌜*He kills Titus.*⌝

LUCIUS
  Can the son's eye behold his father bleed?
                              ⌜*He kills Saturninus.*⌝
  There's meed for meed, death for a deadly deed.
                              ⌜*A great tumult. Lucius, Marcus, and
                              others go aloft to the upper stage.*⌝

MARCUS
  You sad-faced men, people and sons of Rome,
  By uproars severed as a flight of fowl
  Scattered by winds and high tempestuous gusts,   70
  O, let me teach you how to knit again
  This scattered corn into one mutual sheaf,
  These broken limbs again into one body,
  ⌜Lest⌝ Rome herself be bane unto herself,
  And she whom mighty kingdoms curtsy to,   75

78. **But if:** unless; **frosty signs and chaps:** i.e., white hair and cracked skin

81. **erst:** formerly; **our ancestor:** Aeneas, the legendary founder of Rome (See note to 2.3.22.)

82–85. **did . . . Troy:** In Virgil's *Aeneid,* book 2, Aeneas tells the story of the fall of **Troy. sad-attending:** seriously attentive or listening

86. **Sinon:** a Greek who persuaded the Trojans to bring inside the city walls the wooden horse hiding a force of Greek soldiers (See picture, page 200.)

87. **engine:** snare, contrivance (The wooden horse was Troy's **fatal engine.**)

88. **civil wound:** i.e., injury to the city

89. **compact:** composed

93. **move:** persuade; **attend:** listen to, pay attention to

97. **auditory:** audience

101. **fell:** cruel

102. **basely:** i.e., he was **basely; cozened:** cheated

103. **out:** to the finish

Like a forlorn and desperate castaway,
Do shameful execution on herself.
But if my frosty signs and chaps of age,
Grave witnesses of true experience,
Cannot induce you to attend my words,   80
      ⌈*He turns to Lucius.*⌉
Speak, Rome's dear friend, as erst our ancestor,
When with his solemn tongue he did discourse
To lovesick Dido's sad-attending ear
The story of that baleful burning night
When subtle Greeks surprised King Priam's Troy.   85
Tell us what Sinon hath bewitched our ears,
Or who hath brought the fatal engine in
That gives our Troy, our Rome, the civil wound.—
My heart is not compact of flint nor steel,
Nor can I utter all our bitter grief,   90
But floods of tears will drown my oratory
And break my utterance even in the time
When it should move you to attend me most
And force you to commiseration.
Here's Rome's young captain. Let him tell the tale,   95
While I stand by and weep to hear him speak.

LUCIUS
Then, gracious auditory, be it known to you
That Chiron and the damnèd Demetrius
Were they that murderèd our emperor's brother,
And they it were that ravishèd our sister.   100
For their fell faults our brothers were beheaded,
Our father's tears despised, and basely cozened
Of that true hand that fought Rome's quarrel out
And sent her enemies unto the grave;
Lastly, myself unkindly banishèd,   105
The gates shut on me, and turned weeping out
To beg relief among Rome's enemies,
Who drowned their enmity in my true tears
And oped their arms to embrace me as a friend.

111. **her:** Rome's

114. **vaunter:** boaster, braggart

117. **But soft:** an exclamation that means, loosely, "wait a minute" or "listen, be quiet"

119. **For when . . . themselves:** proverbial

125. **is to:** i.e., will

127. **patience:** the capacity to endure

135. **ragged:** rough

136. **mutual closure:** common end or conclusion; **house:** lineage, family line

The Trojan Horse. (5.3.84–88)
From Thomas Heywood, *The Iron Age . . .* (1632).

I am the turned-forth, be it known to you,   110
That have preserved her welfare in my blood
And from her bosom took the enemy's point,
Sheathing the steel in my advent'rous body.
Alas, you know I am no vaunter, I;
My scars can witness, dumb although they are,   115
That my report is just and full of truth.
But soft, methinks I do digress too much,
Citing my worthless praise. O, pardon me,
For when no friends are by, men praise themselves.

MARCUS
Now is my turn to speak. Behold the child.   120
Of this was Tamora deliverèd,
The issue of an irreligious Moor,
Chief architect and plotter of these woes.
The villain is alive in Titus' house,
And as he is to witness, this is true.   125
Now judge what ⌜cause⌝ had Titus to revenge
These wrongs unspeakable, past patience,
Or more than any living man could bear.
Now have you heard the truth. What say you,
    Romans?   130
Have we done aught amiss? Show us wherein,
And from the place where you behold us pleading,
The poor remainder of Andronici
Will, hand in hand, all headlong hurl ourselves,
And on the ragged stones beat forth our souls,   135
And make a mutual closure of our house.
Speak, Romans, speak, and if you say we shall,
Lo, hand in hand, Lucius and I will fall.

AEMILIUS
Come, come, thou reverend man of Rome,
And bring our emperor gently in thy hand,   140
Lucius our emperor, for well I know
The common voice do cry it shall be so.

145. **hale:** drag

146. **adjudged:** awarded judicially; **direful:** dreadful, terrible

151. **aim:** i.e., encouragement (*To give aim*, an expression from archery, means literally to guide an archer in his **aim** by informing him of the outcome of his previous shot.)

152. **heavy:** sorrowful

154. **obsequious:** dutiful; appropriate to a funeral; **trunk:** body, corpse

159. **tenders:** i.e., repays (This sense of the tears and kisses as the discharge of debt continues in **sum** and **pay** in lines 160–61.)

Apollo with his lyre. (4.1.67; 4.3.55)
From Giulio Cesare Capaccio, *Gli apologi* . . . (1619).

⌐ROMANS⌐
    Lucius, all hail, Rome's royal emperor!
MARCUS, ⌐*to Attendants*⌐
    Go, go into old Titus' sorrowful house,
    And hither hale that misbelieving Moor   145
    To be ⌐adjudged⌐ some direful slaught'ring death
    As punishment for his most wicked life.
                        ⌐*Attendants exit. Lucius and Marcus
                            come down from the upper stage.*⌐
⌐ROMANS⌐
    Lucius, all hail, Rome's gracious governor!
LUCIUS
    Thanks, gentle Romans. May I govern so
    To heal Rome's harms and wipe away her woe!   150
    But, gentle people, give me aim awhile,
    For nature puts me to a heavy task.
    Stand all aloof, but, uncle, draw you near
    To shed obsequious tears upon this trunk.
                        ⌐*He kisses Titus.*⌐
    O, take this warm kiss on thy pale cold lips,   155
    These sorrowful drops upon thy ⌐bloodstained⌐ face,
    The last true duties of thy noble son.
MARCUS
    Tear for tear, and loving kiss for kiss,
    Thy brother Marcus tenders on thy lips.
                        ⌐*He kisses Titus.*⌐
    O, were the sum of these that I should pay   160
    Countless and infinite, yet would I pay them.
LUCIUS, ⌐*to Young Lucius*⌐
    Come hither, boy. Come, come, and learn of us
    To melt in showers. Thy grandsire loved thee well.
    Many a time he danced thee on his knee,
    Sung thee asleep, his loving breast thy pillow;   165
    Many a story hath he told to thee,
    And bid thee bear his pretty tales in mind
    And talk of them when he was dead and gone.

171. **latest:** last, final
173. **take leave:** say good-bye to
184. **doom:** sentence

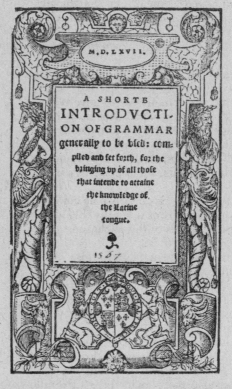

Title page of William Lily's *Grammar* (1567). (4.2.23)

MARCUS

How many thousand times hath these poor lips,
When they were living, warmed themselves on thine!   170
O, now, sweet boy, give them their latest kiss.
Bid him farewell; commit him to the grave.
Do them that kindness, and take leave of them.

YOUNG LUCIUS

O grandsire, grandsire, ev'n with all my heart
Would I were dead so you did live again!   175
⌜*He kisses Titus.*⌝
O Lord, I cannot speak to him for weeping.
My tears will choke me if I ope my mouth.

⌜*Enter Aaron with Guards.*⌝

ROMAN

You sad Andronici, have done with woes.
Give sentence on this execrable wretch
That hath been breeder of these dire events.   180

LUCIUS

Set him breast-deep in earth and famish him.
There let him stand and rave and cry for food.
If anyone relieves or pities him,
For the offense he dies. This is our doom.
Some stay to see him fastened in the earth.   185

AARON

Ah, why should wrath be mute and fury dumb?
I am no baby, I, that with base prayers
I should repent the evils I have done.
Ten thousand worse than ever yet I did
Would I perform, if I might have my will.   190
If one good deed in all my life I did,
I do repent it from my very soul.
⌜*Aaron is led off by Guards.*⌝

LUCIUS

Some loving friends convey the Emperor hence,
And give him burial in his fathers' grave.

198. **weed:** clothing

200. **throw . . . prey:** This fate links Tamora to Jezebel, whom (according to the Bible) God condemned to a similar fate (1 Kings 21.23). The story of Jezebel, the wicked wife of Ahab, King of Israel, is often reminiscent of Tamora's. See 1 Kings 16.29–33, 19.1–2, and 2 Kings 9.30–37. **prey:** i.e., **prey** on

A panther. (1.1.503; 2.2.24; 2.3.195)
From Edward Topsell, *The historie
of foure-footed beastes . . .* (1607).

My father and Lavinia shall forthwith   195
Be closèd in our household's monument.
As for that ravenous tiger, Tamora,
No funeral rite, nor man in mourning weed;
No mournful bell shall ring her burial;
But throw her forth to beasts and birds to prey.   200
Her life was beastly and devoid of pity,
And being dead, let birds on her take pity.

> *They exit,* ⌜*carrying the dead bodies.*⌝

Longer Notes

1.1.69. to yoke: It was a custom among the ancient Romans and others to fashion a symbolic yoke consisting of two spears set upright in the ground with a third on top of them, under which the victors forced their conquered enemies to pass.

69 SD 3, 7. coffin: Both in this stage direction and in the one at 1.1.149, the 1594 Quarto, the basis of our edition, calls for a single coffin, even though the dialogue makes clear that Titus returns with the bodies of more than one dead son (87: "sons"; 122: "brethren"). Perhaps the staging presented in the Quarto is symbolic, rather than realistic. The 1623 Folio also reads *"Coffin"* in the SD at line 69 (to use the line numbering of our edition) but reads *"Coffins"* in the stage direction at line 149.

1.1.138. in his tent: In none of Shakespeare's sources is Polymnestor attacked by Hecuba in Polymnestor's **tent.** In Euripides' *Hecuba*, which was available to Shakespeare in Latin translations, the revenge is carried out in Hecuba's own **tent;** thus some editors change the phrase to read "in her tent." We suggest that the confusion might arise from a misreading of Ovid, which, in the Golding translation, reads "even so Queene Hecubee / . . . too Polymnestor went, / The cursed murtherer, and desyrde his presence too thentent / Too show too him a masse of gold" (ll. 658–62), where Golding's "too thentent" (his normal way of writing "for the intent") can easily be misread as "to the tent." See Barbara A. Mowat, "Lavinia's Message: Shakespeare and Myth," *Renaissance Papers* (1981): 55–69, esp. 59.

1.1.505 SD. **Sound . . . exit.:** As Act 1 ends and Act 2 begins, our edited text brings together the stage direction of the 1594 Quarto and the act division of the 1623 Folio in a manner that calls for explanation. The Quarto, which is not divided into acts or scenes, has Aaron remain onstage at this point—i.e., at the end of what the Folio calls Act 1—so that he can speak at the beginning of the next scene. The Quarto stage direction reads "*Exeunt* [*They exit*]. *sound trumpets, manet* Moore [The Moor stays or remains]." Aaron the Moor then delivers the first speech of what the Folio calls Act 2. While, by today's standards, it would be highly unusual to have a character remain onstage from one act to the next, the Quarto stage direction probably does accurately represent how this play was staged in its own time, the early 1590s. In the outdoor theaters there were no intervals between acts of plays, and few plays for these venues had act divisions at all. Instead, the performance was continuous from beginning to end. By the time the Folio was printed in 1623, theatrical convention had changed and there were act intervals in all playhouses. Thus the Folio changes the Quarto stage direction to read simply "*Exeunt,*" and then, after its "*Actus Secunda,*" prints "*Flourish. Enter Aaron alone.*" (Properly the "*Flourish*" would belong at the end of the first act, where it would signal the exit of the royal couple; properly the Folio should also read "*Actus Secundus,*" but early printed plays are full of such errors, and these therefore need not detain us.)

Since our edition is based on the Quarto, we print its

stage direction, not the Folio's (except for placing its *"Flourish"* at the end of Act 1 and marking it as the Folio's). Since our edition also follows Shakespearean editorial tradition in dividing the play into acts and scenes, we print the Folio's act division. To do otherwise would make act-scene-line numbering incommensurable with that cited by all the scholarship and criticism on the play, thereby severely limiting the usefulness of the edition. It seems worth introducing the anomaly discussed here between Quarto stage direction and Folio act division in order to make our edition more usable.

2.1.93. **Vulcan's badge:** In both Homer's *Odyssey* and Ovid's *Metamorphoses*, **Vulcan's** wife Venus is presented as unfaithful to him by taking Mars as her lover. Horns are the **badge** of the cuckold—the man whose wife is unfaithful—because horns supposedly grow on the cuckold's forehead. See picture, page 52.

2.2.3. **Uncouple:** Titus calls here for the hounds to be set free, and the later stage direction calls for the hounds to bay. Editors disagree about whether real hounds would have been brought onstage; some argue that hounds would have "added to the spectacle here," while others argue that, more likely, players made sounds of barking offstage.

2.3.22. **wand'ring prince and Dido:** There were several popular ballads about **Dido,** including one registered in 1564–65 as "The Wanderynge Prynce." Ross Duffin, in his *Shakespeare's Songbook* (New York: W. W. Norton, 2004), prints two, and argues persuasively that the line "Aeneas, wand'ring prince of Troy . . . ," which begins the second stanza of the earliest surviving manuscript of the *Queen Dido* ballad, was originally the ballad's opening line. Duffin (pp. 321–25) sees Shakespeare's **wand'ring prince and Dido** as an "explicit reference" to this line.

2.3.237. Cocytus' misty mouth: While **Cocytus** refers to a river in the classical underworld of Hades, the phrase **Cocytus' misty mouth** may suggest the hellmouth, or entrance into hell, that was a stage property in Christian cycle drama still performed in the sixteenth century in England.

3.1.10. two-and-twenty sons: At lines 1.1.79–81, Titus gestures toward the surviving four of his "five-and-twenty" sons; this would suggest that he has lost twenty-one sons. Now, in 3.1, Mutius is dead. Titus has thus lost **two-and-twenty sons.** However, Mutius did not die on the battlefield (**honor's lofty bed**) like Titus's other sons. Editors are divided over whether Shakespeare has Titus add Mutius to the list despite the manner of his death or, as Cambridge editor Alan Hughes remarks, "someone has lost count."

4.3.32. But: In the Quarto, this single word appears at the very bottom of the page as the "catchword"— that is, the word that is to appear as the first word on the next page. Instead, the next Quarto page begins "Join with the Goths . . . ," an indication that one or more lines of the play have been lost.

5.2.46. Rape and Murder: When Titus, at 5.2.62, asks Tamora what her companions are called, she answers "Rape and Murder." This later exchange has been interpreted to mean that, at 5.2.46, Shakespeare slipped in having Titus anticipate the answer to his later question. But, as H. F. Brooks suggested, Titus may here give Chiron and Demetrius names that fit the crimes he knows they have committed against Lavinia and Bassianus. In response to Titus's later question, Tamora may simply adopt his earlier names for her sons. After all, Tamora does say (at 5.2.71) that her purpose is to agree with Titus in "his lunacy."

Textual Notes

The reading of the present text appears to the left of the square bracket. Unless otherwise noted, the reading to the left of the bracket is from **Q,** the First Quarto text of 1594 (upon which this edition is based). The earliest sources of readings not in **Q** are indicated as follows: **Q2** is the Second Quarto of 1600; **Q3** is the Third Quarto of 1611; **F** is the First Folio of 1623; **Ed.** is an earlier edition of Shakespeare, beginning with the Second Folio of 1632. No sources are given for emendations of punctuation or for corrections of obvious typographical errors, like turned letters that produce no known word. **SD** means stage direction; **SP** means speech prefix; ~ stands in place of a word already quoted before the square bracket; ʌ indicates the omission of a punctuation mark.

1.1   *Act-scene division in* F; *not in* Q (*Subsequently* F *divides only into acts.*)

    0. SD *Flourish.*] F; *not in* Q

    6. wore] Q (ware)

    9. Romans] Q (Romaines, *and so occasionally hereafter*)

    14. seat, to virtue consecrate,] ~ʌ~~, ~ʌ Q

    18. MARCUS (*aloft, stepping forward and holding up the crown*)] This ed.; *Marcus Andronicus with the Crowne.* Q; *Enter Marcus Andronicus aloft with the Crowne.* F

    23. Piusʌ] ~: Q

24. Rome.] ~, Q
35–36. field. | And now] Q2; field, and at this
day, | To the Monument of that *An-*
dronicy | Done sacrifice of expiation, |
And slaine the Noblest prisoner of the
Gothes. | And now Q
41. Capitol] Q (Capitall)
53. friends,] ~: Q
56. right,] ~. Q
63. SD *Flourish.*] F; *not in* Q
64. SP CAPTAIN] F (*Cap.*); *not in* Q
65. champion,] ~: Q
69. SD *her sons*] Ed.; *her two sonnes* Q
70. weeds!] ~, Q
78. rites] Q (rights)
98. *manes*] Q (*manus*)
98. fleshʌ] ~: Q
122. Goths] *Gotbes* Q
131, 132. Scythia] Q3; Sythia Q
143. rites] Q (rights)
144. entrails] Q (intrals)
151. Rome's] Q (Roomes, *and so occasion-*
ally hereafter)
157. SP LAVINIA] Q3 (*Laui.*); *not in* Q
228. Titan's] Q2 (*Tytans*); Tytus Q
232. SP MARCUS] *Marcus An.* Q
233–35. *Beginnings of lines are damaged in* Q.
235. SD *A . . . down.*] F (*A long Flourish till*
they come downe.); *not in* Q
244. Pantheon] Ed.; Pathan Q
266. chance] Q2; change Q
269. way.] ~ʌ Q
271. hopes.] ~, Q
283. *cuique*] Ed.; *cuiqum* Q
283. justice] iustce Q
302. SD *Enter . . . Moor.*] 2 *lines later in* Q

305. SP SATURNINUS] *Emperour* Q
322. Phoebe] Ed.; *Thebe* Q
323. gallant'st] Q (gallanst)
326. Emperess] Q (Emperesse)
340. queen, to Pantheon.] Ed.; Queene: Panthean∧ Q
344. SD *All . . . exit.*] Ed.; *Exeunt Omnes.* Q
357. hundred] Q (hundreth)
365. SP MARTIUS] Ed.; Q: *Titus two sonnes speakes.*
367. SP MARTIUS] Ed.; *Titus sonne speakes.* Q
369. thee∧] ~. Q
371. struck] Q (stroke)
375. SP QUINTUS] Q (*3.Sonne.*)
376. SP MARTIUS] Q (*2.Sonne.*)
378. SP MARTIUS] Q (*2. sonne*)
386. Ajax] *Ayax* Q
394. SD *Mutius*] Ed.; *him* Q
399. dreary] Q (dririe)
406. F *only; not in* Q
406. SD *Flourish.*] F; *not in* Q
407. SP SATURNINUS] *Saturniue* Q
442. forfend∧] ~. Q
453. throne.] ~, Q
460. raze] Q (race)
484. SP LUCIUS] Ed; *not in* Q; *All.* Q3; *Son.* F
505. SD *Sound . . . exit.*] Ed.; *Exeunt. | sound trumpets, manet Moore.* Q; *Exeunt. | Actus Secunda. | Flourish. Enter Aaron alone.* F

2.1
  4. reach.] ~, Q
  5. sun] suune Q
  25. Holla] Q (Hollo)
37, 46, 62, 77, 94, 99, 103. SP AARON] Q (*Moore*)

63. Goths] *Gotbes* Q
97. struck] Q (stroke)
117. than] Ed.; this Q
125. words.] ~, Q
2.3 1, 30, 52. SP AARON] Q (*Moore*)
11. doth] dorh Q
33. and] ann Q
47. scroll] Q (scrowle)
69. try] Q2; trie thy Q
69. experiments] experimens Q
72. swarthy] Q (swartie)
77. obscure] obsure Q
82. sauciness.] ~, Q
88, 91. SP TAMORA] Q (*Queene*)
106. But] Bu Q
107. yew] Q (Ewghe)
110. Lascivious] Lauicious Q
117. SD *They stab Bassianus.*] Ed.; *stab him* Q (*1 line earlier*)
118. Ay,] Ed.; I∧ Q
118. Semiramis] Q (*Semeranis*)
131. you] Ed.; we Q
132. outlive,] ~∧ Q
140. them∧] ~: Q
144. marble.] ~, Q
150. heard] Q (hard)
158. thee!] ~∧ Q
160. ears] Q3; yeares Q
164. brother] brothet Q
166. will;] ~, Q
172. then?] ~∧ Q
180. satisfy] satisfiee Q
182. womanhood?] ~, Q
192. SD *She exits.*] F; *not in* Q
193. SP AARON] F; *not in* Q
209. SD *He exits.*] Q (*1 line earlier*); *here in* Q2

211. unhallowed] Ed.; vnhollow Q
223. berayed] Ed.; bereaud Q
231. entrails] Q (intrals)
232. Pyramus] Priamus Q
237. Cocytus'] Ed.; *Ocitus* Q
238. out] Q2; our Q

261, 263, 282,
293, 300. SP SATURNINUS] Q (*King.*)
261. grieved] Q (griude)
265. writ,] ~. Q
272. meaning.] ~∧ Q
277. O] Ed.; *King.* Oh Q
286. heard] Q (hard)
286. torturing] Q (tortering)
292, 293. proved] Q (proud, proude)
297. reverend] Q (reuerent)
302. word.] ~∧ Q
305. King.] ~, Q

2.4   2. cut] eut Q
10. SP DEMETRIUS] *Dmet.* Q
11. SP MARCUS] Ed.; *not in* Q
27. him] Ed.; them Q
30. three] Ed.; their Q
55. will] wlll Q

3.1   1. stay.] ~, Q
11. SD *They . . . speaking.*] Ed.; *not in* Q;
Exeunt F (*after line 16*)
21. on] ou Q
23. reverend] Q (reuerent)
33. man.] ~, Q
34. me;] ~, Q
51. pronounced] Q (pronouncst)
69. handless] Q (handles)
148. napkin] Q (napking)
148. with his] Ed.; with her Q

152, 176, 191. SP AARON] *Moore* Q

162. hand.] ~, Q
293. SD *All . . . exit.*] *Exeunt.* Q; *Exeunt.* |
      Manet Lucius. F

3.2   *Scene in* F; *not in* Q
    0. SD *banquet*] *Bnaket* F
    1 *and hereafter in this scene.* SP TITUS]
      Ed.; *An.* F
    8. breast,] ~. F
   13. with outrageous] Ed.; without ragious
      F
   38. mashed] F (mesh'd)
   38. cheeks.] ~, F
   39. complainer] complaynet F
   46. SP YOUNG LUCIUS] Ed.; *Boy.* F
   52. with thy knife] Ed.; with knife F
   53. fly] Flys F
   54. thee,] Ed.; the∧ F
   55. are] Ed.; *not in* F
   57. brother] broher F
   60. How∧] ~: F
   73. myself] Ed.; my selfes F

4.1 1, 7, 16, 43,
108, 113, 119. SP YOUNG LUCIUS] Ed.; *Puer.* Q
   12. Ah] Q3; A Q
   13. Read] Q (Red)
   15. SP MARCUS] Ed.; Q *continues with*
      Titus speaking
   19. griefs] Q (greeues)
   21. sorrow.] ~, Q
   54. Philomela] *Phlomela* Q
   55. Forced] Frocd Q
   64. slunk] Q (slonke)
   79. SP TITUS] Ed.; Q *continues with Mar-*
      cus speaking, repeating his SP at 80; F
      gives lines 78–79 *to Titus.*
   79. Demetrius] *Dmetrius* Q

	89.	hope] Q (hop)
	92.	swore] Q (sweare [*for* "sware"])
4.2	1, 26, 123.	here's] Q (her's)
	4, 8.	SP YOUNG LUCIUS] Ed.; *Puer.* Q
	15.	that] Ed.; *not in* Q
	21.	*nec*] nee Q
	24.	SP AARON] Ed.; Q (*Moore.*)
	53.	Good] Q (God)
	71.	fair-faced] Q (fairefast)
	128.	that] Q3; your Q
	151.	Wheak, wheak] Q (VVeeke, weeke)
	166.	Emperor] Lmperour Q
4.3	32.	But] *catchword at bottom of signature G4v in* Q
	54.	gear.] ~, Q
	58.	Saturn] Ed.; *Saturnine, to* Q
	69, 82, 86.	Jupiter] Q (*Iubiter*)
	78.	SD *a country fellow*] This ed.; the Clowne Q
	79.	News] Ed.; *Clowne.* Newes Q; *Titus.* Newes Q2
	81.	Sirrah] Ed.; *Titus.* Sirra Q
83, 87, 90, 92, 103, 111, 117,	123.	SP COUNTRY FELLOW] This ed.; *Clowne.* Q
4.4	0.	SD *Enter*] *Euter* Q
	4.	equal] Q (egall)
	5.	know, as know] Ed.; know Q
	30.	Th' effects] Q (the 'ffects)
	40.	SD *Country Fellow*] This ed.; *Clowne* Q
	42, 45, 49, 51.	SP COUNTRY FELLOW] Q (*Clowne.*)
	42.	Mistresship] Mistriship Q
	47.	SD *Saturninus reads*] Q (*He reads*)
	51.	By'r] Ed.; be Q

          60. privilege.] ~, Q
          63. SD *nuntius*] *Nutius* Q
72, 82, 97, 107. SP SATURNINUS] Q (*King.*)
          96. feed] Q3; seede Q
         101. ears] Ed.; yeares Q
5.1   0. SD *Flourish.*] F; *not in* Q
           4. desirous] desirons Q
           9. SP FIRST GOTH] Ed.; *Goth.* Q
          13. us.] ~∧ Q
          16. avenged] Q (aduengde)
          17. SP GOTHS] Ed.; *omit* Q
          20. SP SECOND GOTH] Ed.; *Goth.* Q
          43. here's] Q (her's)
          53. Get] Ed.; *Aron.* Get
          54. SP AARON Lucius] Ed.; *Lucius* Q
         112. it?] ~, Q
         115. laughter.] ~, Q
5.2   18. it action] F; that accord Q
          50. globe,] Ed.; Globes. Q
          53. murderers . . . caves] Ed.; murder . . .
               cares Q
          57. Hyperion's] Ed.; *Epeons* Q
          62. Are they] Ed.; Are them Q
          63. so∧] ~. Q
          66. worldly] Q2; wordlie Q
         124. SD *Enter Marcus.*] *1 line earlier in* Q
         146. will] willl Q
         163. it.] ~∧ Q
         199. Procne] Q (*Progne*)
         201. SD *He . . . throats.*] *7 lines later in* Q
5.3   3. SP FIRST GOTH] Ed.; *Got.* Q
          11. SP AARON] Ed.; Q (*Moore*)
          14. inhuman] Q (inhumane)
          15. SD *Sound trumpets.*] *1 line later
               in* Q

17, 25, 30, 39,
41, 48, 53, 60. SP SATURNINUS] Ed.; *King* Q
  36. Virginius] *Viginius* Q
  44. precedent] Q (president)
  46. with] wirh Q
  54. Will't . . . Will't] Q (VVilt . . . wilt)
  64. knife's] Q (kniues)
  65. SP SATURNINUS] Ed.; *Emperour* Q
  74. Lest] Ed.; *Romane Lord.* Let Q
  95. Here's] Q (Her's)
  99. murderèd] murdred Q
 109. oped] Q (opt)
 126. cause] Ed.; course Q
 139. reverend] Q (reuerent)
 143. SP ROMANS] Ed.; *Marcus* Q
 144. SP MARCUS Go] Ed.; Goe Q (*lines
   143–48 given to Marcus*)
 146. adjudged] Q3; adiudge Q
 148. SP ROMANS Lucius] Ed.; *Lucius* Q
   (*Marcus continues speaking.*)
 156. bloodstained] Ed.; blood slaine Q
 165. Sung] Q (Song)
 174. SP YOUNG LUCIUS] Ed.; *Puer.* Q

Appendix: Ovid's Tale of Philomela

From Ovid's *Metamorphoses* 6.561–853,
trans. Arthur Golding (1567)

The sun had now outworn
Five harvests and by course five times had run his
  yearly race
When Progne, flatt'ring Tereus, said "If any love or
  grace
Between us be, send either me my sister for to see,
Or find the means that hither she may come to visit
  me.
You may assure your father-in-law she shall again
  return
Within a while. You do to me the highest great good
  turn
That can be if you bring to pass I may my sister see."
Immediately the King commands his ships afloat to
  be,
And shortly after, what with sail and what with force
  of oars,
In Athens' haven he arrives and lands at Pyrey
  [Piraeus'] shores.
As soon as of his father-in-law the presence he
  obtained
And had of him been courteously and friendly
  entertained,
Unhappy handsel [omen] entered with their talking
  first together.
The errands of his wife, the cause of his then coming
  thither,
He had but new begun to tell and promisèd that when

She had her sister seen, she should with speed be sent
   again

When (see the chance) came Philomel in raiment very
   rich

And yet in beauty far more rich, even like the fairies
   which

Reported are the pleasant woods and water springs to
   haunt,

So that the like apparel and attire to them you grant.

King Tereus at the sight of her did burn in his desire

As if a man should chance to set a gulf of corn [a barn
   bay full of wheat] on fire

Or burn a stack of hay. Her face indeed deservèd love.

But as for him, to fleshly lust even nature did him
   move,

For of those countries commonly the people are above

All measure prone to lechery. And therefore both by
   kind [nature]

His flame increased, and by his own default of vicious
   mind.

He purposed fully to corrupt her servants with reward,

Or for to bribe her nurse that she should slenderly
   regard

Her duty to her mistressward [toward her mistress].
   And rather than to fail,

The lady even herself with gifts he minded to assail

And all his kingdom for to spend or else by force of
   hand

To take her and in maintenance thereof by sword to
   stand.

There was not under heaven the thing but that he
   durst it prove [try],

So far unable was he now to stay his lawless love.

Delay was deadly. Back again with greedy mind he came

Of Progne's errands for to talk, and underneath the
   same

He works his own ungraciousness. Love gave him
     power to frame
His talk at will. As oft as he demanded out of square
     [wrongly],
Upon his wife's importunate desire himself he bare
     [bore].
He also wept as though his wife had willèd that
     likewise.
O God, what blindness doth the hearts of mortal men
     disguise?
By working mischief Tereus gets him credit for to
     seem
A loving man and winneth praise by wickedness
     extreme.
Yea and the foolish Philomel the selfsame thing desires,
Who, hanging on her father's neck with flatt'ring arms,
     requires
Against her life, and for her life, his license for to go
To see her sister. Tereus beholds her wistly [intently]
     though,
And in beholding handles her with heart. For when he
     saw
Her kiss her father and about his neck her arms to draw,
They all were spurs to prick him forth, and wood to
     feed his fire,
And food of forcing nourishment to further his desire.
As oft as she her father did between her arms embrace,
So often wishèd he himself her father in that case,
For naught at all should that in him have wrought the
     greater grace.
Her father could not say them nay, they lay at [urged]
     him so sore.
Right glad thereof was Philomel and thankèd him
     therefore.
And wretched wench she thinks she had obtainèd
     such a thing

As both to Progne and herself should joy and comfort
  bring,
When both of them in very deed should afterward it
  rue.
To endward of his daily race and travel Phoebus drew,
And on the shoring side of heaven his horses downward
  flew.
A princely supper was prepared, and wine in gold was
  set,
And after meat to take their rest the princes did them
  get.
But though the King of Thrace that while were absent
  from her sight,
Yet sweltèd [burned] he and, in his mind revolving all
  the night
Her face, her gesture, and her hands, imagined all the
  rest
(The which as yet he had not seen) as liked his fancy
  best.
He feeds his flames himself. No wink could come
  within his eyes
For thinking ay [always] on her. As soon as day was in
  the skies,
Pandion [father of Philomela and Progne] holding in
  his hand the hand of Tereus pressed
To go his way and, shedding tears, betook him
  [entrusted to him] thus his guest:
"Dear son-in-law, I give thee here (sith [since] godly
  cause constrains)
This damsel. By the faith that in thy princely heart
  remains,
And for our late alliance' sake, and by the gods above,
I humbly thee beseech that as a father thou do love
And maintain her, and that as soon as may be (all
  delay
Will unto me seem over long) thou let her come away,

The comfort of my careful [full of care] age on whom
    my life doth stay.
And thou, my daughter Philomel (it is enough iwis
    [certainly]
That from her father set so far thy sister Progne is),
If any spark of nature do within thy heart remain,
With all the haste and speed thou canst return to me
    again."
In giving charge he kissèd her, and down his cheeks
    did rain
The tender tears, and as a pledge of faith he took the
    right
Hands of them both and joining them did each to
    other plight,
Desiring them to bear in mind his commendations to
His daughter and her little son. And then with much
    ado
For sobbing, at the last he bade adieu as one dismayed.
The foremisgiving [premonition] of his mind did
    make him sore afraid.
As soon as Tereus and the maid together were aboard,
And that their ship from land with oars was halèd on
    the ford [sea],
"The field is ours," he cried aloud. "I have the thing I
    sought."
And up he skipped, so barb'rous and so beastly was
    his thought,
That scarce even there he could forbear his pleasure
    to have wrought.
His eye went never off of her, as when the scareful
    erne [terrifying eagle],
With hookèd talons trussing up a hare among the fern,
Hath laid her in his nest from whence the prisoner
    cannot scape,
The ravening fowl with greedy eyes upon his prey
    doth gape.

Now was their journey come to end; now were they
   gone aland [ashore]
In Thracia when that Tereus took the lady by the hand
And led her to a pelting grange that peakishly [steep-
   roofed] did stand
In woods forgrown [overgrown]. There waxing pale
   and trembling sore for fear,
And dreading all things, and with tears demanding
   sadly where
Her sister was, he shut her up and therewithal
   bewrayed [revealed]
His wicked lust, and so by force because she was a
   maid
And all alone he vanquished her. It booted [helped]
   naught at all
That she on sister, or on sire, or on the gods did call.
She quaketh like the wounded lamb which from the
   wolf's hoar [white, gray] teeth
New shaken thinks herself not safe, or as the dove that
   seeth
Her feathers with her own blood stained, who
   shudd'ring still doth fear
The greedy hawk that did her late with griping talons
   tear.
Anon [soon] when that this mazedness [confusion]
   was somewhat overpassed,
She rent her hair, and beat her breast, and up to
   heavenward cast
Her hands in mourningwise, and said "O cankered
   [corrupt] carl [villain], O fell [savage]
And cruel tyrant, neither could the godly tears that fell
Adown my father's cheeks when he did give thee
   charge of me,
Ne [nor] of my sister that regard that ought to be in
   thee,
Nor yet my chaste virginity, nor conscience of the law

Of wedlock from this villainy thy barb'rous heart
   withdraw?
Behold thou hast confounded all. My sister thorough
   [through] me
Is made a cuckquean [female cuckold], and thyself
   through this offense of thee
Art made a husband to us both and unto me a foe,
A just deservèd punishment for lewdly doing so.
But to th'intent [to the end that], O perjured wretch,
   no mischief may remain
Unwrought by thee, why doest thou from murd'ring
   me refrain?
Would God thou had it done before this wicked rape.
   From hence
Then should my soul most blessedly have gone
   without offense.
But if the gods do see this deed, and if the gods, I say,
Be aught and in this wicked world bear any kind of
   sway,
And if with me all other things decay not, sure the day
Will come that for this wickedness full dearly thou
   shalt pay.
Yea, I myself rejecting shame thy doings will bewray.
And if I may have power to come abroad, them blaze I
   will
In open face of all the world. Or if thou keep me still
As prisoner in these woods, my voice the very woods
   shall fill
And make the stones to understand. Let heaven to this
   give ear
And all the gods and powers therein if any god be
   there."
The cruel tyrant, being chafed [angry] and also put in
   fear
With these and other such her words, both causes so
   him stung

That, drawing out his naked sword that at his girdle
  hung,
He took her rudely by the hair and wrung her hands
  behind her,
Compelling her to hold them there while he himself
  did bind her.
When Philomela saw the sword, she hoped she should
  have died,
And for the same her naked throat she gladly did
  provide.
But as she yearned [cried out], and callèd ay upon her
  father's name,
And strivèd to have spoken still, the cruel tyrant came
And with a pair of pinsons [pincers] fast did catch her
  by the tongue
And with his sword did cut it off. The stump whereon
  it hung
Did patter still. The tip fell down, and quivering on the
  ground
As though that it had murmurèd it made a certain
  sound.
And as an adder's tail cut off doth skip a while, even so
The tip of Philomela's tongue did wriggle to and fro,
And nearer to her mistressward in dying still did go.
And after this most cruel act, for certain men report
That he (I scarcely dare believe) did oftentimes resort
To maimèd Philomela and abused her at his will.
Yet after all this wickedness he, keeping count'nance
  still,
Durst unto Progne home repair. And she immediately
Demanded where her sister was. He sighing feignedly
Did tell her falsely she was dead, and with his subtle
  tears
He maketh all his tale to seem of credit in her ears.
Her garments glitt'ring all with gold she from her
  shoulders tears,

And puts on black, and setteth up an empty hearse
  [templelike structure of wood], and keeps
A solemn obit [funeral] for her soul, and piteously she
  weeps
And waileth for her sister's fate, who was not in such
  wise
As that was for to be bewailed. The sun had in the skies
Passed through the twelve celestial signs and finished
  full a year.
But what should Philomela do? She watchèd was so
  near
That start she could not for her life. The walls of that
  same grange
Were made so high of main [solid] hard stone, that
  out she could not range.
Again her tongueless mouth did want the utterance of
  the fact.
Great is the wit of pensiveness, and when the head is
  racked
With hard misfortune, sharp forecast [plan, scheme]
  of practice entereth in.
A warp of white upon a frame of Thracia she did pin,
And weavèd purple letters in between it, which
  bewrayed
The wicked deed of Tereus. And having done, she
  prayed
A certain woman by her signs to bear them to her
  mistress.
She bore them and delivered them not knowing
  ne'ertheless
What was in them. The tyrant's wife unfolded all the
  clout [cloth],
And of her wretched fortune read the process [story]
  whole throughout.
She held her peace (a wondrous thing it is she should
  so do),

But sorrow tied her tongue, and words agreeable unto
Her great displeasure were not at commandment at
　that stound [time].
And weep she could not. Right and wrong she
　reckoneth to confound,
And on revengement of the deed her heart doth wholly
　ground.
It was the time that wives of Thrace were wont to
　celebrate
The three year rites of Bacchus, which were done a
　nighttimes late [late at night].
A nighttimes soundeth [Mount] Rhodope of tinkling
　pans and pots:
A nighttimes giving up her house, abroad Queen
　Progne trots
Disguised like Bacchus' other froes [priestesses] and
　armèd to the proof [heavily armed]
With all the frantic furniture [costume and equipment]
　that serves for that behoove [the priestess's duty].
Her head was covered with a vine. About her loose
　was tucked
A red deerskin, a lightsome lance upon her shoulder
　rucked [leaned].
In post [haste] gads terrible Progne through the
　woods, and at her heels
A flock of froes. And where the sting of sorrow which
　she feels
Enforceth her to furiousness, she feigns it to proceed
Of Bacchus' motion. At the length she finding out
　indeed
The outset [remote] grange howled out and cried,
　"Now well," and open brake [broke]
The gates and straight [immediately] her sister thence
　by force of hand did take
And, veiling her in like attire of Bacchus, hid her head
With ivy leaves, and home to court her sore amazèd led.

As soon as Philomela wist [realized] she set her foot
  within
That cursèd house, the wretched soul to shudder did
  begin,
And all her face waxed pale. Anon her sister getting
  place
Did pull off Bacchus' mad attire and, making bare her
  face,
Embracèd her between her arms. But she, considering
  that
Queen Progne was a cuckquean made by means of
  her, durst not
Once raise her eyes but on the ground fast fixèd held
  the same.
And where she would have taken God to witness that
  the shame
And villainy was wrought to her by violence, she was
  fain
To use her hand instead of speech. Then Progne
  chafed amain [became very angry],
And was not able in herself her choler to restrain.
But blaming Philomela for her weeping, said these
  words:
"Thou must not deal in this behalf with weeping, but
  with swords
Or with something of greater force than swords. For
  my part, I
Am ready, yea, and fully bent all mischief for to try.
This palace will I either set on fire and in the same
Bestow the cursèd Tereus, the worker of our shame,
Or pull away his tongue, or put out both his eyes, or
  cut
Away those members which have thee to such
  dishonor put,
Or with a thousand wounds expulse that sinful soul of
  his.

The thing that I do purpose on is great, whate'er it is.
I know not what it may be yet." While Progne hereunto
Did set her mind, came Itys [the small son of Progne
    and Tereus] in, who taught her what to do.
She staring on him cruelly, said "Ah, how like thou art
Thy wicked father," and without more words a
    sorrowful part
She purposèd, such inward ire was boiling in her
    heart.
But notwithstanding when her son approachèd to her
    near,
And lovingly had greetèd her by name of mother dear,
And with his pretty arms about the neck had hugged
    her fast,
And flatt'ring words with childish toys [caresses] in
    kissing forth had cast,
The mother's heart of hers was then constrainèd to
    relent.
Assuagèd wholly was the rage to which she erst [at
    first] was bent,
And from her eyes against her will the tears enforcèd
    went.
But when she saw how pity did compel her heart to
    yield,
She turnèd to her sister's face from Itys, and beheld
Now t'one, now t'other earnestly and said "Why tattles
    he
And she sits dumb bereft of tongue? As well why calls
    not she
Me 'sister,' as this boy doth call me 'mother'? Seest
    thou not,
Thou daughter of Pandion, what a husband thou hast
    got?
Thou growest wholly out of kind [nature]. To such a
    husband as
Is Tereus, pity is a sin." No more delay there was.

She draggèd Itys after her, as when it haps in Inde
A tiger gets a little calf that sucks upon a hind
And drags him through the shady woods. And when
   that they had found
A place within the house far off and far above the
   ground,
Then Progne strake [struck] him with a sword—[he]
   now plainly seeing whither
He should, and holding up his hands, and crying
   "Mother, mother!"
And flying to her neck—even where the breast and
   side do bound [adjoin],
And never turned away her face. Enough had been
   that wound
Alone to bring him to his end. Then t'other sister slit
His throat. And while some life and soul was in his
   members yet,
In gobbets they them rent, whereof were some in
   pipkins [small pots] boiled,
And other some on hissing spits against the fire were
   broiled,
And with the jellied blood of him was all the chamber
   foiled [fouled, defiled].
To this same banquet Progne bade her husband
   knowing naught
Nor naught mistrusting of the harm and lewdness
   [wickedness] she had wrought.
And feigning a solemnity [celebration] according to
   the guise
Of Athens, at the which there might be none in any
   wise
Besides her husband and herself, she banished from
   the same
Her household folk and sojourners, and such as
   guestwise came.
King Tereus, sitting in the throne of his forefathers, fed

And swallowed down the selfsame flesh that of his
 bowels [loins] bred.
And he (so blinded was his heart) "Fetch Itys hither"
 said.
No longer her most cruel joy dissemble could the
 queen.
But of her murder coveting the messenger to been [be],
She said "The thing thou askest for, thou hast within."
 About
He lookèd round and askèd where. To put him out of
 doubt,
As he was yet demanding where and calling for him, out
Leapt Philomel with scatt'red hair aflight like one that
 fled
Had from some fray where slaughter was, and threw
 the bloody head
Of Itys in his father's face. And never more was she
Desirous to have had her speech, that able she might
 be
Her inward joy with worthy words to witness frank
 and free.
The tyrant with a hideous noise away the table shoves,
And rears the fiends from hell. One while with
 yawning mouth he proves [tries]
To perbreak up [vomit] his meat [food] again, and cast
 his bowels out.
Another while with wringing hands he weeping goes
 about.
And of his son he terms himself the wretched grave.
 Anon
With naked sword and furious heart he followeth
 fierce upon
Pandion's daughters. He that had been present would
 have deemed
Their bodies to have hovered [humped] up with
 feathers. As they seemed,

So hovered they with wings indeed, of whom the one
    away
To woodward flies, the other still about the house doth
    stay.
And of their murder from their breasts not yet the
    token goeth,
For even still yet are stained with blood the feathers of
    them both.
And he, through sorrow and desire of vengeance
    waxing wight [swift, fleet],
Became a bird upon whose top a tuft of feathers light
In likeness of a helmet's crest doth trimly stand
    upright.
Instead of his long sword, his bill shoots out a passing
    space [a great way].
A lapwing namèd is this bird, all armèd seems his
    face.

Titus Andronicus:
A Modern Perspective

Alexander Leggatt

At the end of Act 2 of *Titus Andronicus* Lavinia enters, *"her hands cut off, and her tongue cut out, and ravished"* (2.4.0 SD). The rapists Chiron and Demetrius come on-stage with her, taunting her: "So, now go tell, an if thy tongue can speak, / Who 'twas that cut thy tongue and ravished thee" (2.4.1–2). They have not only raped her; they have taken her language. In the source myth Shakespeare found in Ovid's *Metamorphoses*, Tereus rapes his sister-in-law Philomela and cuts out her tongue; but she weaves a tapestry that tells her story, and her sister takes revenge. Lavinia has no hands; there is, seemingly, no way she can tell her story. The mutilation also figures externally the shame that attends a raped woman in the play's patriarchal society: Lavinia is now ruined forever. Critics up to the middle of the twentieth century saw *Titus Andronicus* as a pointless horror show, so bad that it was probably not by Shakespeare. But Lavinia's fate has been a key factor in the recent rehabilitation of the play, in the theater as well as in criticism. Violence against women, the denial of women's language—these are issues to which we are now, with good reason, particularly alert; and when Lavinia enters, raped, mutilated, and speechless, it is as though in the middle of a high-flown, consciously literary tragedy someone has pulled a fire alarm.

In our own time, when some act of seemingly random violence hits the headlines—gunfire sprays a school cafeteria, a public building is blown up—we feel both the shock of the unexpected and a grim awareness that the roots of the violence run deep in the society whose peace has just been disrupted. So it is with the rape of Lavinia. The attack takes place in the woods, established as a place of terror outside the bounds of society. Yet looking back, we can see that the act does not come out of nowhere. The rape sequence begins with the two Gothic brothers quarreling over Lavinia, a quarrel Aaron the Moor settles by pointing out that they both can have her. The play likewise began with a competition between two brothers, Saturninus and Bassianus, for the possession of Rome. Bassianus in particular makes Rome sound like a woman whose honor is at stake: "And suffer not dishonor to approach / The imperial seat, to virtue consecrate" (1.1.13–14). Aaron in turn makes Lavinia sound like a captured city, telling Chiron and Demetrius to "revel in Lavinia's treasury" (2.1.139).

The parallel between Lavinia and Rome is strengthened when Saturninus and Bassianus turn from competing for the empire to competing for her. Her father, Titus, makes Saturninus emperor; Saturninus then offers to marry Lavinia, an offer Titus accepts. But she is betrothed to Bassianus, who with the support of the rest of Lavinia's family seizes her and carries her off to marry her. The primary meaning of *rape* in our time is sexual assault, but it can also mean seizure; and in that sense Lavinia is raped twice, once in Rome and once in the woods. Saturninus and Bassianus debate the word, Saturninus declaring "Thou and thy faction shall repent this rape" and Bassianus retorting " 'Rape' call you it, my lord, to seize my own, / My true betrothèd love and now my wife?" (1.1.412–14). Throughout the sequence the emphasis is on Bassianus's rights, and throughout the sequence Lavinia herself is silent. This is not the enforced silence of the second rape, and we could read many different meanings into it. But we have to do the reading, and the parallel has a disturbing effect. Raped and silenced in the woods, she has already been raped and silent in Rome. The atrocity may be not so much an outlaw act as a revelation of the male pride and possessiveness that have already erupted in Rome itself.

Lavinia's father is very much a creature of that male world. The father as well of twenty-five sons, now mostly dead in the wars against the Goths to which he has led them, Titus has spent his life serving Rome. At the start of the play he has returned to bury the latest group of dead sons in the family tomb that exemplifies his standing in Rome and his service to it. He is a creature of habit, his values fixed, his decisions automatic. At the request of his eldest son, Lucius, he sacrifices the Gothic queen Tamora's eldest son, Alarbus, to give the souls of his own sons passage across the Styx. Tamora pleads for her son's life; rejecting her plea, Titus gives no sign that he has even listened to it. He is then given the responsibility of picking the next emperor. Without pausing to think, he chooses Saturninus, simply because he is the late emperor's elder son. He accepts Saturninus's offer to marry Lavinia as an honor done to him, with no thought of Lavinia's feelings or Bassianus's rights. When the rest of the family carries her off he tries to pursue, and kills his own son Mutius for blocking his way, thinking only of the challenge of the moment: "What, villain boy, / Barr'st me my way in Rome?"

(1.1.295–96). Titus is a creature of armor and leather, with thought processes to match.

When Saturninus turns against him and marries Tamora, Titus suddenly feels disoriented, a stranger in the city he thought was his. But it is the return of Lavinia from the woods that breaks him open, presenting him with a sight for which nothing has prepared him, for which no automatic reaction will serve. Marcus, who has discovered Lavinia in the woods and tried to deal with the shock in a long, lyrical speech that turns her wounds into poetry, presents her to her father with the words "This was thy daughter." Ruined and disgraced, Lavinia is finished, no longer a person. Titus's reply, "Why, Marcus, so she is" (3.1.65), restores her to humanity and to relationship. It is as quick as his reactions in Act 1; but those reactions were destructive, and some of them were decisions to kill. This is a decision to keep life going.

Its consequences, however, are far from simple. Titus is now desperate to do something for Lavinia, but when he asks her what he should do, his questions break against silence. (It is part of Lavinia's ordeal that those who are tending her persistently ask her to speak.) Titus offers to create a tableau of grief, the whole family sitting around a fountain until their weeping turns the water salt; he asks if they should cut away their own hands and tongues. His helplessness finally explodes in one unanswerable question: "What shall we do?" (3.1.135). Once a man of action and quick decisions, he can think only of multiplying Lavinia's afflictions in static spectacles. His language expands, giving it a cosmic reach it never had before— but it is filled with images of flood and drowning, images of helplessness.

Aaron fools Titus into cutting off his own hand to save the lives of his sons Quintus and Martius (falsely accused of Bassianus's murder); when in response a messenger enters with the severed hand and the two sons' severed heads, Titus's agony reaches its breaking point. He bursts out laughing. Emotion has gone so far in one direction that it runs into reverse. The laugh is also a turning point for Titus; like a stroke of lightning it clears the air. Tears, he declares, blind his eyes: "Then which way shall I find Revenge's cave?" (3.1.275). The man of action is back; he knows now what he has to do. But there is still nearly half the play to come, and in the tradition of Elizabethan revenge plays (exemplified by Thomas Kyd's *The Spanish Tragedy* [c. 1585] and, with variations, by *Hamlet*) the final deed is held off while the hero, seemingly mad, questions the world that makes revenge necessary. Titus has his relations dig in the earth, fish in the sea, and fire arrows with messages to the gods, all to seek for Justice and to demonstrate that she is nowhere to be found. The answer is revenge. Language was made helpless in the silencing of Lavinia and in Titus's floundering attempts to find the right thing to say to her. Now it is not only restored but linked with violence: Titus sends messages to the court, but he wraps them around weapons. When he captures Chiron and Demetrius, Titus has them silenced (as they silenced Lavinia) and forces them to listen to a long speech in which he outlines their fate: he will cut their throats, bake them in pies, and serve them to their mother, Tamora. Almost literally, he talks them to death.

Titus's revenge, like the act it avenges, has its roots in the myth of Philomela, whose sister Procne feeds Tereus his own son at a banquet. Within the play itself the act is grimly appropriate: Titus will "make two pasties of [their] shameful heads" (5.2.193), recalling the severed heads of Quintus and Martius. He will "bid that strumpet, [their] unhallowed dam, / Like to the earth swallow her own increase" (194–95). Central to the atrocity in the woods is the pit in which Chiron and Demetrius dropped the body of Bassianus, and into which Aaron lured Lavinia's brothers. The pit, like the tomb of the Andronici, is a dark hole that swallows life; now Tamora will be made to imitate it. Quintus also describes the mouth of the pit as stained with blood (2.3.200–202), making it an image of the assault on Lavinia that is taking place as she speaks. The Gothic brothers are entering her body as her own brothers fall into the pit. In revenge Titus compels Chiron and Demetrius to enter Tamora's body, making her the final image of the hole in the earth that swallows men.

That the revenge is imaginatively so like the rape itself may seem to be part of its justice; but it is also part of its horror. It is another turn in a cycle of atrocities from which there appears to be no escape. We may question what relief, if any, it brings Lavinia. Up to a point, she has recovered language. She uses a copy of Ovid, opened at the tale of Philomela, to tell her family she was raped. Coached by Marcus, she puts his staff in her mouth, guides it with her stumps, and writes in the sand the name of the deed and the names of the doers. In one sense she is restored in this moment: she uses language again, and by writing her attackers' names she gains power over them. But to do so she puts Marcus's staff into her mouth, creating a displaced image of the rape itself. She thus describes the rape only at the cost of symbolically reenacting it. The moment recalls one of the play's most disturbing images: at the end of 3.1 Titus places his severed hand in Lavinia's mouth ("Bear thou my hand, sweet wench, between thy teeth"; 287–88). In Titus's tending of Lavinia there has been both genuine affection and a certain invasiveness as he tries to read her thoughts and speak for her. Now that invasiveness is externalized in an image that, like the sight of Marcus's staff in her mouth, reenacts the original atrocity, just as the initial rape in Rome anticipated it.

When in the final scene Titus kills Lavinia, he does so after confirming with the Emperor that the story of Virginius gives him a precedent for his act. Roman honor is satisfied. But what is in Lavinia's mind as her father commands "Die, die, Lavinia, and thy shame with thee, / And with thy shame thy father's sorrow die" (5.3.46–47)? It is easy to assume that Titus is releasing Lavinia from a life that has become intolerable, and that death is what she wants. Some productions stage the scene as a ritual in which Lavinia not only consents but gives the signal for her death. Yet in Titus's act we feel the weight of the patriarchal society he has always served, in which Lavinia earlier seemed to be a pawn. He is preoccupied not with her grief but with her shame; the grief that matters is his own. The last we hear of Lavinia is Lucius's command to bury his father and sister in the family tomb. She is released from an intolerable life, but she is also absorbed into the patriarchal world that was implicated in her suffering.

Titus's revenge, like the rape it avenges, also sends us circling back into Act 1 for a realization that it is not the play's first revenge action. When Tamora pleads for Alarbus, she appeals to her captors as "Roman brethren" and asks Titus to see himself mirrored in her: "And if thy sons were ever dear to thee, / O think my son to be as dear to me" (1.1.104, 107–8). Titus rejects her plea, never acknowledging its force. In Act 2, when Lavinia appeals to Tamora, as one woman to another, to prevent Chiron and Demetrius from raping her, Tamora ignores this appeal to fellow feeling as Titus ignored hers. Tamora has a son to avenge, as Titus will have a daughter. Tamora meets cruelty with cruelty, and Titus will do the same. Disguised as Revenge, Tamora comes to visit Titus, playing on what she thinks is his madness. When Titus welcomes her with a one-armed embrace, the moment has a double significance: Titus is embracing Revenge but he is also embracing Tamora—and the act conveys, more than Titus realizes, how much he and his victim have in common.

Titus has spent ten years fighting the Goths, policing the border of Rome. But in the course of the play, that border becomes remarkably porous; and the distinction between the city and its enemies, between Us and Them, collapses. Titus brings Tamora and her sons to Rome as captives; by the end of Act 1 Tamora is married to Saturninus, installed as Empress of Rome. The enemy is in the citadel. When his son Lucius is sent into exile, Titus makes one of his snap decisions: "Hie to the Goths and raise an army there" (3.1.291). In the last scene Lucius is proclaimed Rome's emperor, charged with restoring Rome and healing its wounds. Yet he has entered at the head of an army of Goths. Restoration is also enemy invasion: again the border has collapsed.

The character who mounts the most telling challenge to any sense of otherness is Aaron the Moor. He appears at first to be the play's ultimate Other: a Moor in the service of the Goths (and how did that happen?), he is doubly foreign in Rome. His blackness sets him apart visually, and his cruel wit gives him detachment of another kind. Telling Lucius of the attack on Lavinia, he describes it as a trip to the barber: "Why, she was washed, and cut, and trimmed; and 'twas / Trim sport for them which had the doing of it" (5.1.96–98). It was Aaron who fooled Titus into cutting off his hand, and helped him do it. He describes the aftermath from his own perspective:

I pried me through the crevice of a wall
When, for his hand, he had his two sons' heads,
Beheld his tears, and laughed so heartily
That both mine eyes were rainy like to his.

(5.1.116–19)

The extravagance of the play's action takes it to the
edge of grotesque comedy. For Aaron, peering through
the wall that signifies his detachment, it *is* a comedy.

Aaron seems not to have noticed that in this scene
Titus laughs too, the laugh that clears away his grief
and turns him to revenge. However, when Titus sends
seemingly mad messages to the court, Aaron is the only
one who notices Titus's wit, and he applauds it. The
play itself moves into Aaron's territory in 3.2, a scene
that appears for the first time in the Folio and may
have been added by Shakespeare as an afterthought.
Marcus casually kills a fly. After Titus rebukes him, in-
voking the grief of the fly's parents, Marcus appeases
his brother by saying "It was a black, ill-favored fly, /
Like to the Empress' Moor. Therefore I killed him"
(67–68). Titus then grabs a knife and stabs away at the
tiny body. Two of the play's key ideas, grief and revenge, spin into absurdity, and the sense of humor at
work is not unlike Aaron's own. Proudly listing his
crimes, Aaron declares "I have done a thousand dreadful things / As willingly as one would kill a fly"
(5.1.143–44). If the fly-killing scene is indeed a later addition, it may have its origin in that line.

When Tamora gives birth to a black baby, the result
of her affair with Aaron, Chiron and Demetrius are
shocked and disgusted. Aaron's response is telling: "He
is your brother, lords" (4.2.126). The line resonates beyond its immediate effect in the scene. It is not so
much a plea for common humanity as a challenge to
recognize in the self the evil that is too easily projected

onto the Other. It brings into focus other such connections: the common ground between Tamora and Titus, the eerie similarity between Lavinia's marriage and her rape, the echoing of Aaron's laughter and Titus's on either side of the wall. Announcing the punishment of Aaron and Tamora at the end of the play, Lucius uses the same phrase, "ravenous tiger," to denounce them both (5.3.5, 197). They are foreign, other, not human. But earlier in the play Titus himself, when the outrages against his family are only just beginning, declares "Rome is but a wilderness of tigers" (3.1.55). The atrocity committed against Lavinia happened outside society, in the wilderness; but the more we reflect on it, the more we find the distinction between Rome and the wilderness dissolving.

Further Reading

Titus Andronicus

Abbreviations: *Oth.* = *Othello*; *Tit.* = *Titus Andronicus*

Bartels, Emily C. "Making More of the Moor: Aaron, Othello, and Renaissance Refashionings of Race." *Shakespeare Quarterly* 41 (1990): 433–54.

  Bartels begins by carefully laying out the representations of Moors as Other in late-sixteenth-century texts before turning to Shakespeare's contributions to this discourse in the figures of Aaron (in *Tit.*) and Othello. She shows how these two major characters are "fashioned from the materials of [Shakespeare's] culture," noting how the differences between Aaron and Othello "reflect the discrepancies and contradictions within those materials." Aaron is "the consummate villain," placed close to the center of power in Rome and given language that links him to the humanistically educated Roman nobles, yet marked, through his unmotivated villainy and through his black skin, as a stereotypically demonized Other. Othello, in contrast, is a valiant general demonized not by *Oth.* but by Iago. Through Iago's manipulation of Othello and those surrounding him, "the play exposes the disturbing power of representation (or misrepresentation) to shape a culture's actions and reactions." At the same time, "it directs our attention to the instability of representation." Showing Iago's use of racial stereotypes to undermine Othello,

Oth. "proves the Moor different not because he has an innate capacity for evil but precisely because he does not."

Dessen, Alan C. *Titus Andronicus*. Shakespeare in Performance Series. Manchester: Manchester University Press, 1989.

Dessen begins by acknowledging the special difficulties facing the historian of performances of *Tit.* The play has posed severe problems for generations of directors, audiences, and readers alike, in part because of its "violent and potentially grotesque moments," and in part because, as a very early Shakespeare play, it suffers by comparison to later masterpieces. Dessen, in studying the play's performance history, focuses on "what has been discovered or realised on the stage" that is not readily available to a reader of the play. He begins by discussing adaptations by Edward Ravenscroft (1678) and by C. A. Somerset and Ira Aldridge in the mid–nineteenth century, as well as the 1923 production by Robert Atkins (1923), before turning to the landmark 1955 production by Peter Brook. He then contrasts stylized and realistic productions since the 1960s, and contrasts cut versions with Deborah Warner's uncut version, produced in 1987 at the Swan in Stratford-upon-Avon and at the Barbicon in 1988. The concluding chapters consider specific production problems presented by this play and the ways directors and actors have handled them. Dessen includes a list of important twentieth-century productions and cast lists for several of the productions discussed.

Fawcett, Mary Laughlin. "Arms/Words/Tears: Language and the Body in *Titus Andronicus*." *ELH* 50 (1983): 261–77.

Fawcett examines *Tit.* "as a meditation on language and the body" and argues that it ought to be used "as a primary text to evolve a theoretical account of the relationship between the body, signs, speech, and writing." Words, such as "arms" and "tears," are "embodied and disembodied throughout [*Tit.*]." Using Lavinia as the "central emblem for both aspects of language," Fawcett explores the juxtaposition of Lavinia's "early muteness" and Tamora's "consistent fluency." Here, "language is split between two poles: it establishes (or seems to establish) identity (Tamora), and it singles out difference (Lavinia)." Ultimately, *Tit.* "finds an abiding conflict between the claims of body and tongue, and an even deeper, and perhaps perverse, alliance between body and writing."

Green, Douglas E. "Interpreting 'her martyr'd signs': Gender and Tragedy in *Titus Andronicus.*" *Shakespeare Quarterly* 40 (1989): 317–26.

Green notes the many ways in which this play parallels other popular revenge plays of the period, but points out that "as is so often the case, Shakespeare touches the limits of the genre and exposes its limitations." Much of that exposure comes in the way the play's two "notable and notorious female characters"—Lavinia and Tamora—are "made to serve the construction of Titus," the play's titanic protagonist. Tamora provides "one pole on the female scale by which we measure Titus," standing sometimes as his direct opposite and sometimes as an illustration of the "extremes of Titus' character," a measure of "the evil to which this patriarchal avenger has resorted and must resort." Lavinia is the other pole of the scale, with her mutilated body articulating Titus's suffering and victimization. Green argues that "as sign, Lavinia is polysemic and disruptive: a sign of the passive suffering attributed to women (like Philomela) by authorities (like Ovid), . . . and a sign beyond complete containment by the patriarchal assumptions of Shakespeare's time— and in some ways our own." In his reading of the play, "gender both marks and is marked by Shakespeare's first experiment in revenge tragedy."

Harris, Bernice. "Sexuality as a Signifier for Power Relations: Using Lavinia, of Shakespeare's *Titus Andronicus.*" *Criticism* 38 (1996): 383–407.

Harris shows how in *Tit.* "representations of virginity, chastity and rape facilitate identifications of authority and function in the construction of gender." She examines how Lavinia's and Tamora's bodies operate "as sites of cultural meaning." As a "changing piece" (1.1.315), Lavinia is a "means by which power is marked as masculine and is then transferred and circulated." Tamora "functions as that feared side of female sexuality: an insatiable sexuality turned loose." Refusing to be owned sexually, Tamora "remains a threat to social order." Harris reads the play so as to "expose and disrupt . . . constructions of gender-specific placements of authority, and uses of a woman's sexual status to determine gender superiority or inferiority."

James, Heather. "Cultural Disintegration in *Titus Andronicus:* Mutilating Titus, Vergil, and Rome." In *Violence in Drama*, ed. James Redmond, pp. 123–40. Themes in Drama 13. Cambridge: Cambridge University Press, 1991.

James meticulously locates *Tit.*'s subtle allusions to Virgil's *Aeneid*, the epic that establishes and celebrates Roman virtues, and explores the implications of Shakespeare's combining these Virgilian references with his obvious allusions to Ovid's *Metamorphoses*, which subverts epic stability in its riot of emotion. The Virgilian allusions early in the play associate Titus with the hero Aeneas, and both Lavinia and Tamora with Dido, queen of Carthage and Aeneas's lover. By Act 2, however, the allusions to Ovid take over, connecting Lavinia to the raped Philomela and, soon thereafter, Titus to the vengeful Procne. James is skeptical about the power of the Virgilian allusion introduced again at the end of the play to return Rome to its heroic past; instead, to her, this allusion is merely a bandage.

Kahn, Coppélia. "The Daughter's Seduction in *Titus Andronicus*, or, Writing Is the Best Revenge." In *Roman Shakespeare: Warriors, Wounds, and Women*, pp. 46–76. London: Routledge, 1997.

Building on the essays by Fawcett, Green, and Willbern listed here and employing an approach that brings together Roman history and feminist psychoanalytical criticism, Kahn identifies *Tit.* as a play about the "politics of sexuality." *Tit.* "positions its hero between a rampaging mother [Tamora] and a dutiful daughter [Lavinia]." For Kahn, Tamora attacks Titus through Lavinia, whose rape and mutilation figure in multiple ways her destruction as a symbol of her father's power. But through his revenge on Tamora—a revenge directed specifically at her threatening motherhood through returning her offspring to the womb from which they came—Titus recovers the power that was once symbolized in Lavinia's integrity.

Kolin, Philip C., ed. *Titus Andronicus: Critical Essays*. New York: Garland, 1995.

Kolin's introduction points out significant trends in the history of *Tit.* criticism and discusses the specific critics identified with these trends. The volume reprints brief extracts from Edward Dowden, *Shakespeare: A Critical Study of His Mind and Art* (1902); Frederick S.

Boas, *Shakespeare and His Predecessors* (1896); H. Bellyse Baildon, ed., *Titus Andronicus* (1904); Eldred Jones, *Othello's Countrymen: The African in English Renaissance Drama* (1965); Leslie Fiedler, *The Stranger in Shakespeare* (1965); Bernard Spivack, *Shakespeare and the Allegory of Evil* (1958); Robert S. Miola, *Shakespeare's Rome* (1983); Gail Kern Paster, *The Idea of the City in the Age of Shakespeare* (1986); and Maurice Charney, *Titus Andronicus* (1990). The following significant critical essays are also reprinted: H. T. Price, "The Authorship of *Titus Andronicus*" (1943); Eugene M. Waith, "The Metamorphosis of Violence in *Titus Andronicus*" (1957); Alan Sommers, " 'Wilderness of Tigers': Structure and Symbolism in *Titus Andronicus*" (1960); A. C. Hamilton, "*Titus Andronicus:* The Form of Shakespearian Tragedy" (1963); David Willbern, "Rape and Revenge in *Titus Andronicus*" (1978); Jane Hiles, "A Margin for Error: Rhetorical Context in *Titus Andronicus*" (1987); Philip C. Kolin, "Performing Texts in *Titus Andronicus*" (1989); Emily C. Bartels, "Making More of the Moor: Aaron, Othello, and Renaissance Refashionings of Race" (1990); Heather James, "Cultural Disintegration in *Titus Andronicus:* Mutilating Titus, Vergil, and Rome" (1991); and Joel G. Fink, "The Conceptualization and Realization of Violence in *Titus Andronicus*" (1989). Five new pieces round out the collection of critical essays: Carolyn Asp's Lacanian " 'Upon Her Wit Doth Earthly Honor Wait': Female Agency in *Titus Andronicus*"; David Bevington's " 'O Cruel, Irreligious Piety!': Stage Images of Civil Conflict in *Titus Andronicus*," a piece that focuses on the play's topicality in the late sixteenth century; Dorothea Kehler's " 'That Ravenous Tiger Tamora': *Titus Andronicus*'s Lusty Widow, Wife, and M/other," which argues that Tamora is a particularly vicious representation of the stereotype of the lusty widow; Philip C. Kolin's " 'Come Down and Welcome Me to This

World's Light': *Titus Andronicus* and the Canons of Contemporary Violence," which sees in the play's "laments over urban violence . . . a play for our age"; and William Proctor Williams's "Courting in Dumb Show: An Editorial and Theatrical Modification in the Text of *Titus Andronicus*," which focuses on how eighteenth-century editors used inserted stage directions to deal with Bassianus's problematic seizing of Lavinia. The section "*Titus Andronicus* on Stage" includes twenty-six reviews, as well as essays by Yoshiko Kawachi on the stage history of *Tit.* in Japan and Horst Zander on *Tit.* in Germany.

Rowe, Katherine A. "Dismembering and Forgetting in *Titus Andronicus*." *Shakespeare Quarterly* 45 (1994): 279–303.

   Rowe, who sees *Tit* as insisting on hands as "the central emblem of effective political action," analyzes the iconographic and discursive traditions of the hand to explore how the dismembered hands of Lavinia and Titus relate to the concept of agency and the political and personal relations in the play. Hands, more than any other body parts, "figure the martial, marital, and genealogical bonds so much at risk in the play." Bringing together Freud's essay "Fetishism" and "the interpretive conventions of the emblem books," Rowe argues that "Lavinia and Titus, in their complex relation to their missing hands," question the " 'natural' associative logic that grounds the faculty of action in the fact of being in a body and having a hand. If dismemberment symbolizes loss of effective action in the world, it is clearly the condition of political agency in the play."

Smith, Molly E. "Spectacles of Torment in *Titus Andronicus*." *Studies in English Literature 1500–1900* 36 (1996): 315–31.

Smith's reading of *Tit.* "focuses on the reciprocal representation of Selfhood and Otherness especially as it manifests itself in depictions of punitive violence." She examines "spectacles of torment" (dismemberment, mutilation, and public execution) and argues that Shakespeare exploits, then deconstructs "the myth of the Other as more violent and horrible than the Self." Smith concludes that the "Self-Other binary" in the play "provides a metacritique of the process of self-definition as inevitably elusive and inadequate."

Tricomi, Albert H. "The Aesthetics of Violence in *Titus Andronicus.*" *Shakespeare Survey* 27 (1974): 11–19.

Tricomi argues that the distinctive importance of *Tit.* lies in the way its "figurative language embodies the events" of its plot, as it "makes the word become flesh." He focuses on "its wittily-obsessive allusions to dismembered hands and heads, and the prophetic literalness of its metaphors," concluding with the figurative language associated with the stage's trapdoor, which functions in the plot as the pit into which Bassianus's body is cast. A typical example of the play's literalizing of its metaphors comes in Aaron's plot to convince Titus to cut off a hand in the hope of ransoming the two of his sons sentenced to death. What Aaron cunningly provides in return for the hand is a metaphor, or more specifically a synecdoche, the figure of speech in which the part stands for the whole, as he restores to Titus the sons in the form of their dismembered heads.

Waith, Eugene M. "The Metamorphosis of Violence in *Titus Andronicus.*" *Shakespeare Survey* 10 (1957): 39–49.

Waith addresses three of the main characters in *Tit.* and finds in their development the influence of Ovid's *Metamorphoses*, which, he argues, has a greater impact on the play than does Senecan tragedy. Observing that Shakespeare's contemporaries read Ovid both in a Christian way for moral allegory and in a pagan way for its stylish narration of "the transforming power of intense emotions," Waith locates the first way in the characterization of Tamora punished through retributive justice for her self-transformation into Revenge, and the second way in the characterization of Titus psychically transformed into vengefulness by grief. Finally, Ovid's style is most prominent in the "psychic distance" that marks the images used by Marcus as he contemplates as an object of wonder the newly raped and mutilated Lavinia—a style, says Waith, best suited to narrative, not drama.

Willbern, David. "Rape and Revenge in *Titus Andronicus*." *English Literary Renaissance* 8 (1978): 159–82.
   In this psychoanalytical exploration, Willbern's topics are "rape and the corresponding reaction of revenge [in *Tit.*] and . . . [the] images and metaphors which sustain this interaction." Initially he associates Rome, Lavinia, and Tamora with each other as maternal figures in danger of attack (rape) and thus in need of defense (revenge). Yet so ambivalent is characterization according to this reading of the play that all three come to be represented by the blood-stained pit in which Bassianus's corpse is discovered; that is, all three become versions of the "dreaded devouring mother"— Rome for its consumption of Titus's sons, Lavinia insofar as her mutilation signals the dangers of sexuality, and Tamora for her terrible vengeance. The only defense against this fantasy of the devouring mother is revenge, and Titus's feeding of her children back into Tamora's womb functions as both rape and revenge.

Shakespeare's Language

Abbott, E. A. *A Shakespearian Grammar.* New York: Haskell House, 1972.

This compact reference book, first published in 1870, helps with many difficulties in Shakespeare's language. It systematically accounts for a host of differences between Shakespeare's usage and sentence structure and our own.

Blake, Norman. *Shakespeare's Language: An Introduction.* New York: St. Martin's Press, 1983.

This general introduction to Elizabethan English discusses various aspects of the language of Shakespeare and his contemporaries, offering possible meanings for hundreds of ambiguous constructions.

Dobson, E. J. *English Pronunciation, 1500–1700.* 2 vols. Oxford: Clarendon Press, 1968.

This long and technical work includes chapters on spelling (and its reformation), phonetics, stressed vowels, and consonants in early modern English.

Houston, John. *Shakespearean Sentences: A Study in Style and Syntax.* Baton Rouge: Louisiana State University Press, 1988.

Houston studies Shakespeare's stylistic choices, considering matters such as sentence length and the relative positions of subject, verb, and direct object. Examining plays throughout the canon in a roughly chronological, developmental order, he analyzes how sentence structure is used in setting tone, in characterization, and for other dramatic purposes.

Onions, C. T. *A Shakespeare Glossary.* Oxford: Clarendon Press, 1986.

This revised edition updates Onions's standard, selective glossary of words and phrases in Shakespeare's plays that are now obsolete, archaic, or obscure.

Robinson, Randal. *Unlocking Shakespeare's Language: Help for the Teacher and Student.* Urbana, Ill.: National Council of Teachers of English and the ERIC Clearinghouse on Reading and Communication Skills, 1989.

Specifically designed for the high-school and undergraduate college teacher and student, Robinson's book addresses the problems that most often hinder present-day readers of Shakespeare. Through work with his own students, Robinson found that many readers today are particularly puzzled by such stylistic devices as subject-verb inversion, interrupted structures, and compression. He shows how our own colloquial language contains comparable structures, and thus helps students recognize such structures when they find them in Shakespeare's plays. This book supplies worksheets—with examples from major plays—to illuminate and remedy such problems as unusual sequences of words and the separation of related parts of sentences.

Williams, Gordon. *A Dictionary of Sexual Language and Imagery in Shakespearean and Stuart Literature.* 3 vols. London: Athlone Press, 1994.

Williams provides a comprehensive list of the words to which Shakespeare, his contemporaries, and later Stuart writers gave sexual meanings. He supports his identification of these meanings by extensive quotations.

Shakespeare's Life

Baldwin, T. W. *William Shakspere's Petty School*. Urbana: University of Illinois Press, 1943.
   Baldwin here investigates the theory and practice of the petty school, the first level of education in Elizabethan England. He focuses on that educational system primarily as it is reflected in Shakespeare's art.

Baldwin, T. W. *William Shakspere's Small Latine and Lesse Greeke*. 2 vols. Urbana: University of Illinois Press, 1944.
   Baldwin attacks the view that Shakespeare was an uneducated genius—a view that had been dominant among Shakespeareans since the eighteenth century. Instead, Baldwin shows, the educational system of Shakespeare's time would have given the playwright a strong background in the classics, and there is much in the plays that shows how Shakespeare benefited from such an education.

Beier, A. L., and Roger Finlay, eds. *London 1500–1700: The Making of the Metropolis*. New York: Longman, 1986.
   Focusing on the economic and social history of early modern London, these collected essays probe aspects of metropolitan life, including "Population and Disease," "Commerce and Manufacture," and "Society and Change."

Bentley, G. E. *Shakespeare's Life: A Biographical Handbook*. New Haven: Yale University Press, 1961.
   This "just-the-facts" account presents the surviving documents of Shakespeare's life against an Elizabethan background.

Chambers, E. K. *William Shakespeare: A Study of Facts and Problems*. 2 vols. Oxford: Clarendon Press, 1930.

Analyzing in great detail the scant historical data, Chambers's complex, scholarly study considers the nature of the texts in which Shakespeare's work is preserved.

Cressy, David. *Education in Tudor and Stuart England.* London: Edward Arnold, 1975.

This volume collects sixteenth-, seventeenth-, and early-eighteenth-century documents detailing aspects of formal education in England, such as the curriculum, the control and organization of education, and the education of women.

Dutton, Richard. *William Shakespeare: A Literary Life.* New York: St. Martin's Press, 1989.

Not a biography in the traditional sense, Dutton's very readable work nevertheless "follows the contours of Shakespeare's life" as he examines Shakespeare's career as playwright and poet, with consideration of his patrons, theatrical associations, and audience.

Honan, Park. *Shakespeare: A Life.* New York: Oxford University Press, 1998.

Honan's accessible biography focuses on the various contexts of Shakespeare's life—physical, social, political, and cultural—to place the dramatist within a lucidly described world. The biography includes detailed examinations of, for example, Stratford schooling, theatrical politics of 1590s London, and the careers of Shakespeare's associates. The author draws on a wealth of established knowledge and on interesting new research into local records and documents; he also engages in speculation about, for example, the possibilities that Shakespeare was a tutor in a Catholic household in the north of England in the 1580s and that he played particular roles in his own plays, areas that reflect new, but

unproven and debatable, data—though Honan is usually
careful to note where a particular narrative "has not
been capable of proof or disproof."

Schoenbaum, S. *William Shakespeare: A Compact Documentary Life*. New York: Oxford University Press,
1977.
   This standard biography economically presents the
essential documents from Shakespeare's time in an accessible narrative account of the playwright's life.

Shakespeare's Theater

Bentley, G. E. *The Profession of Player in Shakespeare's
Time, 1590–1642*. Princeton: Princeton University Press,
1984.
   Bentley readably sets forth a wealth of evidence
about performance in Shakespeare's time, with special
attention to the relations between player and company,
and the business of casting, managing, and touring.

Berry, Herbert. *Shakespeare's Playhouses*. New York:
AMS Press, 1987.
   Berry's six essays collected here discuss (with illustra-
tions) varying aspects of the four playhouses in which
Shakespeare had a financial stake: the Theatre in Shore-
ditch, the Blackfriars, and the first and second Globe.

Cook, Ann Jennalie. *The Privileged Playgoers of Shakespeare's London*. Princeton: Princeton University Press,
1981.
   Cook's work argues, on the basis of sociological, economic, and documentary evidence, that Shakespeare's
audience—and the audience for English Renaissance
drama generally—consisted mainly of the "privileged."

Greg, W. W. *Dramatic Documents from the Elizabethan Playhouses*. 2 vols. Oxford: Clarendon Press, 1931.

Greg itemizes and briefly describes many of the play manuscripts that survive from the period 1590 to around 1660, including, among other things, players' parts. His second volume offers facsimiles of selected manuscripts.

Gurr, Andrew. *Playgoing in Shakespeare's London*. 2nd ed. Cambridge: Cambridge University Press, 1996.

Gurr charts how the theatrical enterprise developed from its modest beginnings in the late 1560s to become a thriving institution in the 1600s. He argues that there were important changes over the period 1567–1644 in the playhouses, the audience, and the plays.

Harbage, Alfred. *Shakespeare's Audience*. New York: Columbia University Press, 1941.

Harbage investigates the fragmentary surviving evidence to interpret the size, composition, and behavior of Shakespeare's audience.

Hattaway, Michael. *Elizabethan Popular Theatre: Plays in Performance*. London: Routledge and Kegan Paul, 1982.

Beginning with a study of the popular drama of the late Elizabethan age—a description of the stages, performance conditions, and acting of the period—this volume concludes with an analysis of five well-known plays of the 1590s, one of them (*Titus Andronicus*) by Shakespeare.

Shapiro, Michael. *Children of the Revels: The Boy Companies of Shakespeare's Time and Their Plays*. New York: Columbia University Press, 1977.

Shapiro chronicles the history of the amateur and quasi-professional child companies that flourished in

London at the end of Elizabeth's reign and the beginning of James's.

The Publication of Shakespeare's Plays

Blayney, Peter W. M. *The First Folio of Shakespeare.* Hanover, Md.: Folger, 1991.

Blayney's accessible account of the printing and later life of the First Folio—an amply illustrated catalog to a 1991 Folger Shakespeare Library exhibition—analyzes the mechanical production of the First Folio, describing how the Folio was made, by whom and for whom, how much it cost, and its ups and downs (or, rather, downs and ups) since its printing in 1623.

Hinman, Charlton. *The Norton Facsimile: The First Folio of Shakespeare.* 2nd ed. New York: W. W. Norton, 1996.

This facsimile presents a photographic reproduction of an "ideal" copy of the First Folio of Shakespeare; Hinman attempts to represent each page in its most fully corrected state. The second edition includes an important new introduction by Peter W. M. Blayney.

Hinman, Charlton. *The Printing and Proof-Reading of the First Folio of Shakespeare.* 2 vols. Oxford: Clarendon Press, 1963.

In the most arduous study of a single book ever undertaken, Hinman attempts to reconstruct how the Shakespeare First Folio of 1623 was set into type and run off the press, sheet by sheet. He also provides almost all the known variations in readings from copy to copy.

Key to Famous Lines
and Phrases

These words are razors to my wounded heart.
[*Titus*—1.1.320]

He lives in fame, that died in virtue's cause.
[*Lucius*—1.1.398]

She is a woman, therefore may be wooed;
She is a woman, therefore may be won.
[*Demetrius*—2.1.86–87]

. . . what you cannot as you would achieve,
You must perforce accomplish as you may.
[*Aaron*—2.1.113–14]

The hunt is up, the moon is bright and gray,
The fields are fragrant, and the woods are green.
[*Titus*—2.2.1–2]

The birds chant melody on every bush,
The snakes lies rollèd in the cheerful sun,
The green leaves quiver with the cooling wind
And make a checkered shadow on the ground.
[*Tamora*—2.3.12–15]

What fool hath added water to the sea
Or brought a faggot to bright-burning Troy?
[*Titus*—3.1.70–71]

THE FOLGER SHAKESPEARE LIBRARY

The world's leading center for Shakespeare studies presents
acclaimed editions of Shakespeare's plays.

All's Well That Ends Well

Antony and Cleopatra

As You Like It

The Comedy of Errors

Cymbeline

Hamlet

Henry IV, Part 1

Henry IV, Part 2

Henry V

Henry VI, Part 1

Henry VI, Part 2

Henry VI, Part 3

Henry VIII

Julius Caesar

King John

King Lear

Love's Labor's Lost

Macbeth

Measure for Measure

The Merchant of Venice

The Merry Wives of Windsor

A Midsummer Night's Dream

Much Ado About Nothing

Othello

Pericles

Richard II

Richard III

Romeo and Juliet

Shakespeare's Sonnets

Shakespeare's Sonnets
and Poems

The Taming of the Shrew

The Tempest

Timon of Athens

Titus Andronicus

Troilus and Cressida

Twelfth Night

The Two Gentlemen of Verona

The Winter's Tale

Three Comedies: The Taming
of the Shrew/A Midsummer
Night's Dream/Twelfth Night

Three Tragedies: Hamlet/
Macbeth/Romeo and Juliet

For more information on Folger Shakespeare Library Editions, including
Shakespeare Set Free teaching guides, visit www.simonsays.com.

SIMON & SCHUSTER
PAPERBACKS
A CBS COMPANY